RACE PRIDE
SCHOOL PRIDE

SAMI ATIF

Books & Things Publishing, LLC
4410 Brookfield Corporate Dr. #220149
Chantilly, VA 20153

RACE PRIDE SCHOOL PRIDE
Text copyright © 2025 Sami Atif
Cover design by Butter Bird Design
Interior Design and format by Books & Things Publishing, LLC
First Edition November 2025
ISBN 978-1-962140-43-0
ISBN 978-1-962140-44-7
Library of Congress Control Number: 2025922198

To schedule author events or order in bulk, visit the Books & Things Publishing website at www.booksandthingspublishing.com.

CONTENTS

INTRODUCTION

I am still not sure how to tell this story. For a long time, I worried that it had become too personal — a musing brought on by my unique circumstances. I made several attempts, as the saying goes, to let sleeping dogs lie, or to pass the responsibility of documenting it on to colleagues, journalists, alumni, and even students. In hindsight, my insecurities as a writer, researcher of history, and storyteller fueled much of this doubt. In truth, this is not my story to tell. I lack, in this case, the feelings one holds for an alma mater. I am merely a close observer, an insider with an outsider's sentiment. I am in it, but I am not of it.

The following is a book about school, pride, and the making of both. For what would school be without pride? At times, I will present exact answers, pose rhetorical questions, and suggest detours for others to pursue. But as I relay this story, I approach it as I would a first day of class. I hope you will join me as I explore the contours of how racial pride and school pride evolve in concert. What I offer for you to consider is a living case study compiled from multiple archives and the oral histories of two schools. It originates with the founding of the United States of America and spans the twenty-first century. It is a story of regional interest, for sure. It is niche, but the implications are much broader. I pray that it will be a remedy for what presents as all too well and a reminder of our core morbidity as a society. For those with unanswered questions about school, or if you have not been taught to question school, then this story is especially yours.

I have a habit of purchasing more books than I have the time to read. But in the late winter of 2022, after months of sitting idle, I began Bobby Lovett's *America's Historically Black Colleges and Universities: A Narrative History, 1837–2009*. I can not exactly recall how I came to find Lovett's book, but I am certain it sits along a lifelong journey of self-discovery. My most vivid memories involving race include the awakening of self-pride and the confrontation of so many lies. In Philadelphia, I attended racially diverse yet predominantly white magnet schools for my middle and high school years. While most schools are zoned for a particular section of the city, magnet schools are public schools designed to attract the best and brightest city-wide. Outside of school, my family, neighborhood, religious upbringing, interests, and activities were unapologetically Black. I was told that education was the method of upward mobility, and I believed it. My academic success was a source of family pride. I also took pride in disproving stereotypes about Black students. But as I excelled in the classroom, my world became less and less Black, and I lost motivation. That is, until I followed my eldest brother to Cheyney University, recognized as the United States' first Historically Black College and University (HBCU). I was finally able to be at school and let my guard down, to simply learn.

At Cheyney, I discovered a tangible use for my affinity with mathematics. As a lead tutor and the only student majoring in my field of secondary education, I was suddenly *the math guy*, whereas previously I was one of *the only* Black students in a math class. To receive such personal acknowledgment and to perceive the universal indictment on Black people was sobering. I knew it was a racist idea that Black people could not do math. I also recognized that far too many Black people were convinced that they could not do math. And I was soon to discover that the entire concept of doing math was a lie. With the mentorship of Black professors and the camaraderie of classmates, displaying grit and work ethic — the pull yourself up by your bootstraps arguments for academic success — became a question of individual circumstance, not dismissive racist rhetoric. Speaking on my HBCU experience at Cheyney and later at Delaware State University, I felt the warm-demanding embrace. I learned to show up for myself. I also showed up to make my mother proud, and I showed up because so many could not. More emphatically, I showed up because so many wouldn't allow anything less. There are more than 100 different HBCUs with countless attendees, employees, and their families; I was certain that my story was a common one. I came to Lovett's work wondering just how common, and why so.

Less than thirty minutes into reading, a familiar dissonance gave me pause when I encountered the name Fessenden. A family name with Saxon origins, it is also the name affixed to my place of employment: The Fessenden School, located just outside of Boston in West Newton, Massachusetts. But here, in Lovett's book, Fessenden referred to Fessenden Academy, a school based in Martin, Florida, with a vital history tied to Black education. And this very dilemma halted my reading. For the longest time, I had held Black schools and the network of elite independent schools in parallel yet distinct mindsets. And I stress parallel. I understood that race, wealth, and education not only stratify people but also suggest hierarchies when no real difference exists. For me, a name that could have been easily overlooked grabbed my attention with an unrelenting curiosity.

In the process of contextualizing the founding of several HBCUs, Lovett drew attention to the work of the American Missionary Association (AMA). It was here that Florida's Fessenden Academy, listed as one of the many secondary schools the AMA sponsored, caught my eye. Still, it was more than a glitch in recognition that caused my initial shock. For more than a century, The Fessenden School, my employer, had served privileged white males almost exclusively. I was thoroughly taken aback. A Black Fessenden school stood in stark contrast against the curated narrative and widely accepted image of American prestige and scholarly pursuit. It shocked my senses and reopened a conflict of consciousness. Was this my latest confrontation with a half-truth, another hidden Black first? Or was it an example of our similarities if race, power, and intolerance did not steal away our potential?

As a career educator, I live to dismantle the unjust narratives I once encountered as a student, and this is my place of entry. A journey that began with reading has led to writing, and pursuing answers has produced more questions, extending the path. To be sure, this book is not the destination, and of this, I am certain. When I shared parts of this story with the Black boys in Boston, I could sense them adopting a new effect. Their backs straightened, and I felt their focus. Exuding confidence, one boy asked — what felt more like a demand — "When will you tell everyone else?!" Teachers will recognize that when a student calls for a broad message in this fashion, they are expressing personal frustration and offering a group assessment. His response speaks to the racial awareness of all students and the default identity of the school. Of the many outcomes for this project, I am most excited to see how current generations of Fessenden students remember, enact, and shift the paradigm.

In February 2023, I visited Florida in the wake of a national discussion over the state's newly enacted Individual Freedom Act, commonly known as the Stop WOKE (Wrongs to Our Kids and Employees) Act. Passed by a Republican state legislature and signed into law by Governor Ron DeSantis, the law purports to protect children from a grab-bag of wrongs, but what kind of wrongs does the law concern, and which kids are shielded from harm? Along with the irony of attempting to legislate public schoolrooms and corporate boardrooms, the bill amended Florida's Civil Rights Act of 1992 to prohibit indoctrination inconsistent with one's individual freedom. Critics point to this as an attempt to silence and counter what they would call social progress. But the governor's office's desire to "take on corporate wokeness and critical race theory" reeks of political signaling rather than sound policy.

Interestingly enough, woke and critical race theory are two faces on a set of dice that constitute Black political thought and resistance as I know it. Said another way, my woke friends have little to do with critical race theorists or practitioners. The love for Black people runs consistent, but the space each group occupies, their tactics, proximity, and audience have less in common than this bill assumes. A law that simultaneously polices the language of barbershops and Black academia is indeed racist. It would be uncommon for jurisprudence to enter a *woke conversation* without being dismissed as a primary tool to oppress Black people. And should that conversation proceed after citing the many battles waged within the courtroom to deny Black people their humanity and eventually the legal victories that brought about any semblance of equality in this land, one might reference the poet, activist, and feminist writer, Audre Lorde: "For the master's tools will never dismantle the master's house. They may allow us to temporarily beat him at his own game, but they will never enable us to bring about genuine change."

For some, there is no entry point to appreciate what it means to work or attend a predominantly white independent school. The sight of sprawling fields, manicured lawns, and brick buildings on what can appear like a small liberal arts college campus is inviting. Small class sizes with the latest technology at every child's fingertips and classmates from around the world model a progressive learning environment. Often, I am asked, "Are there any Black students? How many? What about Black teachers? How much does it cost?" It is a struggle to make it make sense unless you know. As I take a deep breath before responding, I know I have a better chance of simplifying differential calculus than I have of explaining the tragic promise of privatized education. For all the opportunities that exist in being of the selected few, the cost for many of us can be even greater.

When I reunite with Black graduates from my previous independent schools, I often ask, "Was it worth it? Would you do it again? Would you send your children?" Below the surface of these questions rests an appreciation for how damaging the experience can be. For the fortunate few who appear unscathed and well-adjusted, their upward mobility and social capital have certainly required a prolonged centering of whiteness. Implicitly or otherwise. The questions then become, *How does one find a balance between racial pride and school pride? Is it even possible?*

Following the *Brown v. Board of Education* decision in 1955, famed Floridian Zora Neale Hurston opined, "The whole matter revolves around the self-respect of my people." Quite unpopular at the time, Hurston's critique speaks to the very tension. Hurston continues, "But if there are adequate Negro schools and prepared instructors and instructions, then there is nothing different except the presence of white people."

Today, decisions around school choice are indeed complex. A family's financial forecast and the student's learning profile are key drivers in the discussion of school choice. In cases where the presence of white people implies the presence of resources, Hurston's words are an important reminder that, as she says, "it is a contradiction in terms to scream race pride and equality while at the same time spurning Negro teachers and self-association." Like many of my former students, self-reflective individuals grapple with it all.

As a graduate of two Historically Black Colleges, Cheyney University of Pennsylvania and Delaware State University, I know well how school pride and racial pride align almost uniformly. While many Black graduates of historically white schools seek to balance their school pride and racial pride, there is something unapologetic among the alums of Black schools. In general, placing a singular value on education is inherently unjust. The promise of an HBCU education or Black schools at large is belonging. These institutions are not without their shortcomings. But, whereas many private white schools have expanded from diversity to inclusion, to equity, to belonging, to community, and even to justice in recent years, the work has been cosmetic at worst and gradual at best. Now in 2025, even these gestures face legal scrutiny and the full weight of partisan politics.

The attempt to remedy a white-majority institution, to elevate belonging or community as a concept everyone should aspire to, risks fostering a kind of disharmony. One who is marginalized is encouraged to feel like a member of an already exclusive group. But, in that pursuit, someone or something must compromise. In this way, belonging and community rarely inspires a group, let alone a legacy institution, to change, though the individual reorients years before applying. Seeking elite membership is more like pledging a fraternity. But when a group belongs to you, there is no trial period, no fitting in. Your seat is reserved. There is something waiting for you to inherit, something you already own. I will not romanticize entitlement, hierarchy, and privilege, even amongst oppressed people. If freedom includes possessing viable choices, then actively deciding where to study is an act of resistance. A pathway was laid for me to receive an education at Cheyney and Delaware State. And a pathway was laid for me to teach at Phillips Exeter Academy and The Fessenden School. However, Black scholarship was modeled for me at my HBCUs, and we understood that standard as the rule. Not the exception. The pride I feel in upholding the rule is not the same as pride in being the exception.

The narrative in the coming chapters is full of important protagonists, some with Fessenden surnames and others, mostly Black, whose names appear on no school buildings. The backdrop, of course, is American racism. In the face of physical violence, psychological terror, and intellectual hypocrisy, the existence of a Black community evokes pride, be it in Massachusetts or Florida. The self-determination that we will see in Florida has the same spirit of resistance as the organizing efforts of Black families throughout Boston and its surrounding towns. With this lens, I can appreciate a Black affinity group at a white institution as a striving community removed from circumstance. The exact condition of overt racism and legal segregation that made Black schools necessary has only morphed over time. In its wake, the failures in American education are both understandable and full of regret. If pride plays an important role in education, so does shame.

Feeling powerful or powerless is an extreme motivator for all human behavior, including scholarly pursuit, and especially in the formation of narrative. When we mask emotion or remove feelings from the academic discourse, we commit a disservice to all students. Often reduced to gender and racial bias, cognition has become the inheritance of some, and in particular, white males. Even when we teach their great works with an intellectual framing alone, we have lied. Much of what I learned about discovery and enlightenment proved to be aggrandizing. History certainly is not only a collection of facts and events; pride and shame have everything to do with what is remembered. My heart never sat quite right with the idea that Black people were not of the first, or were not of global significance, or did not operate with agency in their affairs. So, despite my footing in The Fessenden School of Massachusetts, my grounding was in something very different. Academic curiosity has not brought me this far. A deep desire to liberate myself and to connect Black students intergenerationally led me to Florida.

In the spring of 2023, the National Association of Colored People (NAACP) Board of Directors issued a formal travel advisory for Florida. Citing the governor's public statements and current legislative record, the notice reads: "Florida is openly hostile toward African Americans, people of color, and

LGBTQ+ individuals. Before traveling to Florida, please understand that the state of Florida devalues and marginalizes the contributions of and the challenges faced by African Americans and other communities of color." When I traveled in February 2023, this was foreseeable. I felt the uneasiness in many places—indeed, Florida teachers and my relatives expressed as much. But when I visited the Fessenden Elementary School, something was different. The Marion County public school, situated on the same grounds as the historic Fessenden Academy, served as a safe haven for learners amid open hostility.

After weeks of emailing, phone calls, and checking social media, I secured an invitation from the Fessenden Alumni Association for their Black History Month Reunion. I was now heading to Martin, Florida, from Boston. President of the Association, Johnny Grimes, extended the invitation with a request to deliver the keynote address. Without hesitation, without knowing the audience or what made me suitable, or what I would say, I agreed. While seemingly a modest engagement, the magnitude, for me, was undeniable. These two Fessenden schools have existed in utter isolation for more than 120 years. Bridging the distance of time, space, race, and class was an existential thrill, along with an exercise in diplomacy.

As I stood ready to speak to the audience of Fessenden Academy alumni, I caught sight of four middle-aged white women seated close by—the only non-Black attendees. They were stationed just right of the podium, in an area sectioned off for special guests. The superintendent of Marion County Schools joined three local school board members. Later, I discovered that the Alumni Association had tactfully invited government officials to attend their Black History Month event. Recognizing that many were pro-DeSantis constituents, the need to acquiesce to transparency outweighed the political threat. There were also ongoing attempts to close the school, of which I was unaware. Despite Fessenden's designation from the Department of the Interior as a National Historic Landmark, budgetary concerns about the aging campus jeopardized the school's future. In hindsight, I would have declined the offer to speak if I had known how carefully I needed to choose my words. The risk was simply too high.

However, in my direct sightline were Black men and women old enough to be my parents, grandparents, or elders. They were alums, former teachers, children of alums, siblings to alums who could not make the journey, current faculty, administration, and retirees. They had lived with these external threats for generations. They knew that their school was a special place, and they came together to commune with one another. "We came," as one graduate stated, "to remember the past, to enrich the future." At the Fessenden school in Massachusetts, I am a teacher, and for that I am grateful. At the Fessenden school in Florida, I am a student, and for that I am equally grateful. So, in a large fieldhouse-sized gymnasium, organized in rows of chairs spaced for social distancing, I was invited into an intimate space, and we had a conversation. One that gave me balance. One that restored. One that I will remember.

Fessenden Academy and High School Reunion, February 2023, Marion County, Florida. From right to left, Whitfield Jenkins, Loretta Jenkins, Sami Atif, Johnny Grimes, and Demoris Rhodes.

CHAPTER 1

Naming is an intentional gesture that serves to build pride or remove it. Consciously or not, what we call a thing determines how future generations will remember it. Memories play their own dual role. They can be suppressed, erased, or neglected; or, they can recover and center. Choosing what to remember, in what context, and in relation to one's self is then, also intentional. This is pride.

During the summer of 2020, I became the first Director of Equity and Inclusion at the Fessenden School in West Newton, Massachusetts. In my childhood, I attended public school in Philadelphia, an unlikely precursor to an executive administrative position at a New England independent school. In New England, independent schools, like many universities, are historically white institutions, from faculty to students, founded with the implicit purpose of exclusively training white students to succeed in college and in life. The Fessenden School (grades pre-K-9), located in a wealthy suburb bordering Boston, and Phillips Exeter Academy (grades 9-12), my previous employer, located in rural Exeter, New Hampshire, are just two examples. The former was founded in 1903 by Frederick James Fessenden with the stated mission of preparing young boys for the rigors of attending the latter. Throughout the period of legalized segregation in the United States and beyond, a Fessenden-Exeter-Harvard University education formed a closed circuit conferring elite status. Each institution branded by a shade of crimson or red, we can think of these schools as ideological descendants of one another, as breeding grounds for the scions of wealth and a pathway to power. It is therefore understandable that one could fail to see a Fessenden tradition of social justice and Black liberation. Whether lost to time or neglect, the story of how Black people encountered members of the Fessenden family is one worth recovering, and to do so, we must find a common entry point.

Throughout the 1970s, Massachusetts Senator Edward Kennedy's support of the Civil Rights Act of 1957 and the subsequent establishment of the United States Commission on Civil Rights provides a link between these two grade schools. Although identical in name, they are separated by a thousand miles and more than one hundred years of history. Director of the Commission John Allen Buggs, appointed by three successive presidents, would partner with Senator Kennedy in the 1970s to help implement the act and monitor its effects. Senator Kennedy and Director Buggs would have fond memories of their Fessendens: equally proud environments in which to learn, though fundamentally different. Exploring the dichotomy of these schools through the frame of each leader offers a clear case study of race and education in America.

In 1942, at the age of twenty-seven and nearly two decades before being appointed Director of the Commission on Civil Rights, John Buggs was named director of the historically Black boarding school known as Fessenden Academy in Martin, Florida. This same year, a young Ted Kennedy would enroll at the historically white, all-male boarding school, The Fessenden School, in West Newton, Massachusetts. For the general public, Fessenden is a peculiar name that is less recognizable than many other colonial-era family names. Therefore, a school carrying the

Fessenden name would have less meaning and comparably little context compared to the more popular Washington and Lincoln schools across the country. However, for Director Buggs, Senator Kennedy, their intimate circle of peers, and those in the know, Fessenden is both classic and unmistakable.

These private schools reveal an essential story about our similarities and our differences. Respectively, the Fessenden schools were no less critical to the social milieus in which they operated. They both played key roles in binding a community together and shaping its leaders. Each thrived off the loyalty and deep devotion of its student body and family networks. Yet, the contrasts in the resources and legacies are stark. In this space filled with competing images, memories, and narratives, what follows gives context for a most unlikely encounter. This is not a conventional telling of one family's history. Nor is it a comprehensive study of each Fessenden school. Our focus here is on how Black people experience school and why. Before we can appreciate how young minds were fashioned on different sides of the color line, within distinct class structures, and in geographically different regions, we need to ask a particular set of questions. First among them: who are the Fessendens, and how were they known to Black people?

****

In 1628, King Charles of England granted a charter that paved the way for the Massachusetts Bay Company to colonize the lands between the Charles and Merrimack rivers and initiate trade. Like other colonial joint-stock companies, the Massachusetts Bay Company was a corporate and governmental entity that tied self-governance and religious freedom to financing, contracts, and repayments. The Puritans, or the Reformers as they preferred to be called, comprised most of the company. Historian James T. Adams offered a fitting description for the earlier Plymouth territory: "The Bible and the beaver were two mainstays of the young colony. The former saved the morale, and the latter paid its bills."[1]

It did not take long for New England to model itself after old England by adopting a system of free, forced labor to enrich itself. Originally silent on the issue of slavery, the colonies nevertheless relied on European ideas and customs to shape their society. In 1641, the colony's first constitution legalized the enslavement of war captives.[2] Two years later, motivated by a desire to control the region's fur trade, the colonists banded together with other Native tribes to overcome the Pequot Indians, who were estimated to be a population of several thousand before European arrival, smallpox, and war decimated their nation. The remaining captured Pequot became the first enslaved people of New England. The enslaved Pequot Indians were bartered eventually for enslaved Africans and other goods from the West Indies.[3] The trading of furs, lumber, and agriculture created an economic base for the survival of the colony. Over time, as the slave trade expanded, the infrastructure at ports, textile mills, schools, law offices, print houses, and churches facilitated exponential profits.

The Puritans believed in a separation of church and state, but not in a separation of state from God. They came to replicate the austerity of their homeland and to require church membership, public attendance, and taxes to support church maintenance and salaries.[4] Dissenters, including Quakers and Baptists in their eyes, were threatened with death for public preaching or with banishment to England or nearby areas.[5] By 1648, the Cambridge Platform — attributed to Puritan ministers Richard Mather and John Cotton and considered the religious constitution of New England — formalized the Congregational church polity as the law of the land.[6] Faith remained a central frame throughout this period. Even the catastrophic decline of Native communities, caused by the pathogens brought by early European traders, was purported by Puritan priests as a sign that God had prepared the land for pilgrims.[7] The entire project of colonization centered on both profit and praise.

The exact date of the Fessendens' arrival in North America is unclear. By 1638, John and Jane Fessenden were the first of their family to settle in Cambridge, Massachusetts Bay Colony. As a non-indentured freeman and land-owning member of the church of Cambridge, John amassed considerable wealth and distinction, working as a glover and periodically serving as selectman for the town from 1656 until his death in 1666. Having no heirs, it is believed that John and Jane made a special request for other Fessenden family members living in England to join them to inherit their property and wealth. Arriving as young children between 1660 and 1665, Nicholas and Hannah Fessenden became the primary beneficiaries of their uncle John and aunt Jane.[8]

Hannah Fessenden married John Sewall, the brother of prominent judge Samuel Sewall, and, from their union, had seven children.[9] The Sewall line contains a number of antislavery jurists and lawyers that we will revisit later. After John's passing, Hannah remarried Lt. Jacob Tappan, the great-great-great uncle of abolitionist Lewis Tappan. We will see later a connection between the Fessenden and Tappan lineages. Nicholas

Fessenden married Margaret Cheyney. Their eleven children, who all lived to adulthood, comprise what is understood to be the origin of the Fessenden family tree. That is to say, over the past three-and-a-half centuries, any Fessenden living in America would most likely have Nicholas as their common ancestor.

Nicholas followed his uncle's profession as a glover, tanner, and crafter of various animal hides and skins. In 1682, Nicholas inherited the bulk of the family estate. Given what we know about the time, he would have also adopted the beliefs of the Congregational Church. In general, religion served as the moral authority guiding one's life, and Congregational doctrine preserved the independence of smaller, newer, localized churches and other more established congregations from interference by the Church of England.[10] However, for congregants, their personal, religious, and governmental lives were very much interdependent. The first generation of Nicholas's descendants remained close to Cambridge and took respective careers in farming, carpentry, tanning, academia, and the ministry. Among the male heirs were graduates of Harvard College and at least one schoolmaster.

The Fessendens would have been in close proximity to the important debates and noteworthy figures of the era. For the Puritans of colonial Massachusetts, few leaders were more prominent than Cotton Mather. By the 1700s, Mather's writings on Christian theology and jurisprudence were among the most widely circulated in the British colonies. Having more than four hundred printed works to his credit and ministering to a church of hundreds of followers, the scale of Cotton Mather's impact is without dispute.[11] Carrying the names of two influential families

— John Cotton and Richard Mather — his story has become something of a legend, drawing both praise and criticism.

The Salem Witch Trials remain a notorious event. In 1692, Cotton Mather's opinion was sought after by the court, and he joined figures including Judge Samuel Sewall, brother-in-law to Hannah Fessenden, in a spectacle that accused over two hundred individuals — mostly women — of witchcraft, resulting in the hanging of nineteen. While not directly presiding over the verdict, Mather's writing was used to justify the rulings of Sewall and others.[12] Similarly, Mather's pro-slavery statements were well-known. In 1706, an African man was gifted to Cotton Mather by his congregation in Boston. Mather writes: "Some gentleman of o(u)r church, understanding I wanted a Good Servant...purchased for me a very likely Slave; a Young Man, who is a Negro, of promising Aspect and Temper." As a student of the Bible, Mather chose the name Onesimus, which translates to useful one, for his enslaved servant. "I put upon him ye name...and I resolve, with ye help of ye Lord...to make him a servant of Christ."[13]

However, Onesimus was not his actual name; it was erased and remains unknown. Mather was keen to witness his conversion to Christianity, and his worldview left no room for Onesimus to self-actualize or to contribute anything of value outside of labor. Mather wanted to prove that he, of all people, could convince his slave to follow his religion. The irony of all ironies is Mather's conviction that he could save the soul of his enslaved and, thereby, demonstrate to the colonists the religious redemption of all Africans.[14] However, it was Onesimus, the enslaved, who would save the literal lives of colonizers. When the smallpox epidemic of 1721 threatened to wipe out the population of Boston, an African healing technique — taken from Onesimus by Mather — saved the city.[15] Even today, the inoculation performed in pre-colonial Western Africa isn't given the mantle of medical sophistication. And during Onesimus's time, it took the threat of plague and increasing death tolls to force Mather to reason with his peers and steer them away from their deep racial prejudice and accept the validity of a proven procedure. In that moment, Mather is either the hypocritical upholder of slavery or a devout Christian blinded by so much religious hubris that he can not see the contradictions inherent in his practice.

Mather wrote persuasively to his fellow colonists on the virtue of converting enslaved people to Christianity, arguing that teaching English to one's slave for the purpose of conversion was a benevolent act. Furthermore, he wrote quite emphatically that, "the baptized, then, are not thereby entitled to their liberty." Which was to say directly to slaveholders that their investment would not be jeopardized and that owning a literate Christian was not blameworthy in the eyes of the court nor in the eyes of God. Indirectly, Mather's argument suggests that Africans were worthy of bondage because of how Europeans saw their race and intelligence, not their religion. In his 1706 essay, *The Negro Christianized*, Mather uses demeaning language to describe Black people in general: *stupidity, barbarity, their complexion,* and the *wretched Negro* to name a few. And follows with, "the vast improvement that education has made in some of them argues that there is a reasonable soul in all of them…they are men, not beasts that you have bought, and they must be used accordingly…Christianity will be the best cure."

Centuries later, ideas of racial hierarchy and gestures toward religious paternalism can be observed most clearly in what students learn. Black students are not allowed to be individuals. Instead, they represent the ultimate potential or demise of the race. In this way, Black education carries the legacy of this supposedly virtuous endeavor: to prove the individual worthiness of Black people and to display the nobility of wealthy benefactors. Mather's rhetoric helps form an arc of repression that has tried to circumscribe the experience of Black students for the country's entire history. It has failed to do so, but a tremendous price has been paid. After years of effort, Mather also failed to convince Onesimus to convert. Mather acknowledged that his former slave was "pretty intelligent," but also regarded his refusal to embrace the Christian faith as a character flaw. By 1716, Mather agreed to the terms of Onesimus's freedom, which Onesimus lobbied to attain: produce the money necessary for a replacement slave, reimburse Mather for the lost time he spent earning wages elsewhere, and complete daily tasks at the Mather home without pay.[16]

We could travel in many directions with questions about Onesimus. Beyond acknowledging his individual story, the Mather family for whom he labored, his biological family, never to be seen again, and all the loss he endured, Onesimus is not singular. He reminds us of others who have been diminished to human chattel. The Trans-Atlantic Slave Trade removed tens of millions of African people from a diverse continent containing thousands of distinct tribes and nations, each with its own language, religion, and customs, and reduced them to a single group: negro or slave. But, more specifically, Onesimus, biblically known to the Puritans as a slave who converted to Christianity and returned to his master, would have been an attractive name for one's slave, but a pejorative nonetheless. Exactly how many enslavers followed Mather in selecting this name for their human property is unknown. At the time, Mather's status was unrivaled, but Boston city records note at least two enslaved individuals bearing the same name in the 1720s. Later church records show that Rev. Joseph Sewall, son of Judge Sewall, wedded a man named Onesimus to a Black woman named Jane.[17] A separate account states that an unrelated enslaved Onesimus married a woman named Hagar, and came to baptize three children, one of whom was also named Onesimus. Then, in 1759, a "free negro" Onesimus, perhaps the child just mentioned, married Phillis, a negro servant to Rachel Fessenden.[18]

Rachel Fessenden was born Rachel Gatte and, in 1749, became engaged to Nicholas Fessenden, the fourth child of Nicholas and Margaret. Little is known about the life that Phillis led under bondage. Marriages between free and enslaved Africans often resulted in great toiling and longing to live as a free family. As a result, the already dire circumstances of negotiating freedom became even more compromised and exploitative. It is clear from this account that the degrees of separation between educated, land-owning church members and the institution of slavery were indeed few. However, for the Fessenden family, public records, including wills and the details captured in *The Fessenden Family in America*, contain no reference to slaveholding. As members of the Cambridge Church, it is possible that the future generations of Fessendens favored the position of Judge Samuel Sewall over the more popular Cotton Mather. In 1700, six years prior to Mather's *The Negro Christianized*, Sewall published what is considered to be the first anti-slavery essay in New England entitled *The Selling of Joseph*. Speaking to his fellow colonists, Sewall decries slavery and argues that Africans are "the offspring of God." While maintaining white cultural supremacy and the separation of the races, Sewall refutes any notion that slavery is moral.[19]

Slavery in New England was not a lesser form of bondage tempered by legal proceedings, religious dogma, virtuous owners, noble educators, and academic jousting. Like elsewhere, enslaved people opposed their condition at every turn. A few years before the wedding of Onesimus and Phillis, we have the story of Mark and a different enslaved woman, also named Phillis. "Thursday last, in the afternoon, Mark, a negro man, and Phillis, a negro woman, both servants of the late Captain John Codman, of Charlestown, were executed at Cambridge, for poisoning their said Master," read the September 22, 1755 *Boston Evening Post*. "The fellow was hanged, and the woman burned at the stake…they both confessed." In the mind of enslavers and colonizers, acts of rebellion could not go unpunished, certainly not the murder of a notable white citizen. The report continues: "After execution, the body of Mark was brought to Charlestown Common and hanged in chains, on a gibbet, erected for that purpose."[20] Mark and Phillis desired freedom. For their actions, Phillis became only the second woman in New England burned at the stake, and Mark's body remained as a terrorizing symbol, chained to a post for more than twenty years. Decades later, in a 1798 account of his famous Midnight Ride at the outset of American independence, Paul Revere would casually mention a well-known landmark, "where Mark was hung in chains," as a site along his journey to alert colonists that British soldiers had invaded.[21]

The sheer brutality warrants a pause to emote. Then consider how normal it must have been for the governing elites to argue that one race of people was worthy of freedom while using all manner to subjugate another. Our ability to reimagine the public discourse in its entirety and, more importantly, individual lives, is somewhat limited. For the average early European immigrant turned colonizer, including the Fessendens, we have mostly silence in the face of slavery. To what degree was slaveholding something of personal disdain? Were individuals willing participants in or complacent with the status quo, and if so, would they, in hindsight, acknowledge complicity? These are just some of the burning questions, the very thoughts that drum up internal shame and cause paralysis. The shame at the root of book bans is the same emotion that advances ahistorical beliefs, delays justice, and presides over a deafening silence. Thankfully, somewhere along my educational journey, I learned to center Black people, and that tutelage allowed me to read the Fessenden family narrative in a different context.

As the Revolutionary War approached, colonists continued to expand into the North American territories west and north. One particular branch of the Fessenden family ventured forward and, within a few generations, left a lasting legacy. Born in 1718, William Fessenden of Cambridge is the grandson of Nicholas and Margaret. His father, also William, was born in 1694 and assumed the family trade as a carpenter and a tanner. William, the grandson, graduated from Harvard College in 1737 and became a schoolmaster and preacher. His son, also named William, was born in 1747 and is the great-grandchild of Nicholas and Margaret. William, the great-grandson of Nicholas, graduated from Harvard in 1768 and thereafter studied medicine and theology. By 1775, William was the lead minister for a group led by Joseph Frye encroaching further into native lands.[22]

A veteran politician and commander during the French Indian War (1754-1763), Colonel Joseph Frye leveraged his service to his fellow countrymen and the potential for profits in his petition to the Massachusetts government. He sought control over the lands far north of the Massachusetts colony known to the indigenous tribes as Pequawket. Frye described the region near the Saco River as a "considerably good settlement" and believed that inhabiting the lands would "render them more valuable to the Government." Approved in 1762, the official land grant stipulated that Joseph Frye would take *sixty good families*, dedicate land for a school, and "forever" use a Protestant minister.[23] But before William Fessenden (b.1747) would receive his call to the ministry, it was Limbo, an enslaved Black man, who would be one of the first to settle on the land.

What we know about Limbo's life is greatly overshadowed by what has been lost: his full birthname, details of his life before chattel slavery, his words, and dreams. We can remember Limbo because those who came to occupy the land that we call Maine thought enough of him to preserve their memories for later generations. "Any account of the Pequawket settlement would be incomplete without the story of Limbo, the slave, who, even in this remote northern locality, was a factor in American civilization," reads a 1898 family account by Simeon A. Evans.[24] Limbo, kidnapped from his home near the coast of Guinea, survived the horrific sea journey known by some as the Middle Passage and was sold to enslavers in the area of Gorham, Maine. From there, along with Nathaniel Merrill and John Stevens, Limbo drove livestock and other provisions during the bitter seasons in 1762 and 1763 to a settlement that would become Fryeburg. Limbo did not return to Gorham. Instead, it is reported that Limbo was inspired by a group of *come-outers and new-lights* — Christian settlers who believed that slavery was a sin and therefore abandoned any church that was not committed to abolition. Limbo may have been the earliest pioneer on Maine's expanding Underground Railroad. Eventually, the harsh conditions in the mostly uninhabited wilderness made recapture as difficult as living there.

It remains unclear what brought Limbo back into bondage or when. It may have been capture or surrender, or the confounding factors of his age or state of isolation. In comparison, around 1765, another enslaved man of the town, Abel Cary, freed himself only to return from the wilderness weeks later. Limbo certainly met with ill-treatment upon his return. Under Moses Ames, another early settler in Fryeburg, Limbo's treatment brought such notable shame that by 1790, Col. Samuel Osgood, moved by compassion, purchased Limbo for a yoke of oxen. A subsequent sale between father and son placed Limbo's rights under the discretion of Lt. James Osgood, and a future bequest bonded Limbo to the Osgood family for decades to come. Whether he sought freedom again is unknown. After a lifetime of labor, whatever decency Limbo was afforded to move about the town's people and within the Osgood home would have been earned. Eventually, at the age of ninety in 1828, Limbo became free of this life. His grave, which still stands today, is marked by a plaque in the town's historic cemetery. It reads: Limbo, a native of Africa, lies here. He was, while living, an honest man, The noblest work of God.[25]

Ministering requires a great deal of intimacy and proximity with one's congregation. Rev. Fessenden was beloved by his congregants, and they compensated him for his efforts. At the outset of the Revolutionary War, Rev. William Fessenden expressed a desire to join the war effort. At the time, the territories of Maine were under the jurisdiction of the Massachusetts colony. Colonists either joined a local militia or served multiple years with the Continental Army. However, church members voted unanimously for their reverend to remain in service of the town's people. Newer settlements required close family ties and shared responsibility in order to survive. As the first pastor of Fryeburg, Rev. Fessenden would have witnessed business transactions, officiated church ceremonies, aided with political organizing, and consulted on academic endeavors. In 1791, Rev. Fessenden, Moses Ames, Simon Frye, James Osgood, and others petitioned the Courts for financial aid to build a school. The Massachusetts Courts responded with a land grant of several hundred acres. Serving as trustees, the group founded Fryeburg Academy in 1792.[26] Twenty years later, while attending Fryeburg Academy, the son of Rev. Fessenden and the soon-to-be vocal antislavery proponent Samuel Fessenden, befriended Daniel Webster, the future U.S. Secretary of State. The two would remain friends for fifty years until the cause of abolition made matters irreconcilable.

Closer to Boston, the grandchildren of Nicholas and Margaret Fessenden would have encountered the public debates around abolition. Prior to the late 1700s, there was little political will in the Massachusetts legislature to outlaw the practice of chattel slavery. However, one of the most direct pathways available to enslaved people in colonial Massachusetts to liberate themselves from bondage was to make a legal claim for freedom. These court filings stand in stark contrast to runaway slave advertisements. In them, we hear the voice of the enslaved, not the enslaver. In the face of moral hypocrisy, some petitioners were successful in blending logic with the Bible and the law to gain their freedom. Prince Hall, a prominent leader in Boston's free Black community and a member of the Congregational Church, began organizing for abolition as early as 1773. Previously enslaved to William Hall of Boston, he shared the profession of tanning with many Fessendens. An advocate for Black servicemen and a patriot of the Revolutionary War, in 1777, Prince Hall used the language of the Declaration of Independence to plead for statewide abolition. He wrote, "the petition of us…held in a state of slavery within the bowels of a free country." [27] Hall's demand for justice was effectively ignored for six years until 1783, when the Massachusetts Supreme Court finally decided that *all men are created equal* and *certain unalienable rights, endowed by their Creator,* implied freedom for Black people.

Manumission in Massachusetts alone did very little to end overt racism or the practice and profit of slavery more generally. For example, in 1788, following an incident where three Black men were abducted from Boston Harbor, taken to the West Indies, and sold, Hall again petitioned on behalf of a *great number of freemen* for Massachusetts to enact laws preventing the slave trade within the commonwealth.[28] The mere existence of some Northern sympathies with slaveholding and obvious financial ties to the slave-based economy of the South was the undercurrent to a very public devaluing of Black life in nineteenth-century Boston. Even after abolition, free Blacks were subject to extra-judicial murder, kidnapping, illegal sale, and an atmosphere of Black inferiority codified by what white people learned in school. Black Bostonians, led by Prince Hall, organized to demand citizenship rights, labor rights, and, explicitly for quality education. As we will see often, schools were one of the first institutions Black Americans sought with their freedom.

Following the 1783 statewide abolition of slavery, Boston's free Black population considered themselves to be equal citizens, but much like Hall's earlier 1777 antislavery petition was ignored, white Bostonians slow-walked citizenship rights, including the right to public education. The message was clear and unwelcoming: be free, but far from here. Lead author of the Declaration of Independence (1776), future U.S. Secretary of State (1789), and U.S. President (1801), Thomas Jefferson's *Notes on the State of Virginia* was published in 1781 and influenced public opinion throughout the country. In addition to degrading the intelligence of Black people, Jefferson recommended "great allowances for the difference of condition, of education, of conversation, of the sphere they move."[29] While enslaving an average of 130 people at any given moment, totaling six hundred for his lifetime, Jefferson argued that the best solution for the dilemma of free Black people in America was African Colonization, i.e., to send them back. Boston, Massachusetts, was home to the largest free Black population at the time, and this community pioneered the fight for equality under the law and quality education in the classroom. Truthfully, Black students were not welcomed into the public schools because they were not wanted as citizens in the society.[30]

Which children learn in a society is as consequential as what children learn. Few topics have sparked a more contentious debate or elicited deeper feelings than this. One cannot fully understand education in the U.S. without an appreciation for how Christianity, racism, and classism operate. Black citizens who inherit a painful legacy of being the only legally commodified and economically disenfranchised group in American history have consistently demanded equal, not even equitable, distribution of public funds for public education. Met with no repair, but rather, denial, history is full of Black efforts to self-fund and garner private investment when the government failed to live up to its own ideals. Hence, while it may be tempting to suggest that Black people choose separate schools for their children, even this corrupts the narrative and distorts the viewpoint.

Founded in 1635, Boston Latin School is this nation's oldest public school and represents the colonists' commitment to basic education for future generations. The 1647 pronouncement from the Massachusetts General Court made schooling compulsory in the colony and included rules for taxing *the parents or masters of such children*, or *the inhabitants in general* per town.[31] Nearly a century and a half later, with the country independent from the crown and Black Bostonians emancipated, public schools legally had to make room for Black children, but did so with little accommodation. The experience with racism, hostility, and rudimentary lessons led Prince Hall and fourteen others to petition for a separate school in October of 1787, in which he stated that Black youth, "receive no benefit from free schools in the town of Boston." These tax-paying freemen cited their children's mistreatment for "no other reason can be given...than they are black," and requested that the Massachusetts General Court make provision for their children.[32] The request, which would have been the first separate but equal school ruling in U.S. history, was denied.

The exact reasoning behind the state's refusal to fund a separate Black school is debatable. What is undeniable is the conditions that Black students encountered in Boston's public schools. Matters did not improve, and as the nineteenth century approached, the problem worsened as the city's free population climbed from roughly seven hundred to twelve hundred. The epicenter of this community rested on the steep northern slope of Beacon Hill, a section of Boston that was home to Prince Hall and other luminaries such as abolitionist writers David Walker and Maria Stewart. This area, full of historical markers today, emerged as the pulpit for abolition and a major terminal for the Underground Railroad. It began as undesirable land facing the harbor and open to freezing winds and the smell of a busy shipping industry. The characteristic tight alleyways and small homes were features of the working poor, and it was what free Black people could afford and where they were allowed. For much of the 1800s it was colloquially called Nigger Hill. Most unfortunately, hate-filled language did not escape the children. Hosea Easton, renowned Congregationalist minister, writer, and schoolteacher, in 1837 stated, "negro or nigger is an opprobrious term, employed to impose contempt upon them as an inferior race, and also to express their deformity of person." He continued to describe the sentiment in schools where students, "are threatened with being made to sit with the niggers, if they do not behave." Easton was clear to point out something that escaped many Bostonians: banning slavery was a step, "but prejudice is destructive to life."[33] In this light, we can better understand Hall's 1798 revived petition, this time to the city of Boston, requesting a separate school to avoid *discord* — racism, and to prepare Black children for citizenship, and perhaps why they chose the African School as a name.

The Boston School Committee rejected the request for funding, and in response, Black parents pooled their resources and opened the African School on their own in 1798.[34] One of the reasons for the city's denial was demographics, and who took priority when it came to spending public funds. White Bostonians were not a monolith; there were wealthier families of the church, political, and business elite whose children historically received private lessons or attended private schools — the type of families who lived on the other side of Beacon Hill, on the south side, facing the State House and Boston Common. There were also growing populations of generational white day laborers and more recent immigrants. Hall's 1798 request came at a time when white citizens were demanding extensions to the public school system to include lower-income white children. Should the Irish, Scot Irish, French, and German also have separate schools was a debated question. And this fueled resentment: the feeling of "discriminating in favor of Black youth at the possible expense of native, white children."[35] Decision-makers failed to see the merits; worse, they were blind to the intellectual inconsistency. Even some clergymen expressed that Black Bostonians should be content with their current station in life. In reality, most Black people struggled at the lowest rung of the social ladder. Unemployment was high, and few Black parents were in the position to make a formal request for quality schools, let alone pay for one. Boston's free Black community suffered from economic starvation that forced many children into the workforce and away from public schools.[36] For those Black leaders who could speak proudly and loudly for themselves, they were neighbors to those who could not. Despite anyone's claim, Black parents didn't seek a segregated school; they wanted a school free of racism. The African School is therefore the best example of what most consider to be an independent school.

The pursuit of a quality school experience was central to many of the efforts this community undertook throughout the 1800s. This spirit of togetherness led to the creation of several notable Black institutions that continue to thrive today. Before the American Revolution, Prince Hall was initiated into the British Army lodge for Freemasons. After the war ended, he and his brothers were denied a charter by the Americans, which led Hall to procure an English charter in 1784. The African Lodge or Prince Hall Freemasonry became a cornerstone, providing social status. As the community grew, forty-four men organized the Boston African Society in 1796, a mutual aid organization pledging monthly dues, spiritual well-being, care during illness, decent burial, and support for widows.[37] Social life for Black Bostonians revolved around racial upliftment and the abolition of slavery. Other organizations adding to that fabric included the Colored Men's Debating Society, the Afro-American Female Intelligence Society, and the American Union for the Relief and Improvement of the Colored Race. A Black middle class began to take root in Boston's West End neighborhood, adjacent to Beacon Hill. Seeking a new building in which to worship, twenty-four members of the African Baptist Church, fifteen of whom were women, raised funds to erect the African Meeting House in 1805. This historic site served as the gathering space for the religious, cultural, political, and educational needs of the community.[38] For twenty-seven years, the African School held classes on the bottom floor of the Meeting House. However, the school's first location was in the home of Prince Hall's eldest son, Primus, a war veteran, freemason, church founder, and educator.

The story of the African School is rich with important lessons about self-determination, Black political thought, allyship, and most certainly education. For our case study, that is the two Fesseden schools, terms like public, private, and independent have nuanced meanings, which we will explore more closely. We will also consider which students and families were sought after, who the teachers were, and what the curriculum contained in later chapters. Here, I will make the argument plain and straightforward. Based on how the country's founders used the word "independence" and how Europeans understood formal education, the African School, free from racial tyranny and in protest against taxation without representation, is America's first independent school. We understand American independence as freedom not simply from control or the ability to self-manage, but a response to an oppressive government. Each of the nearly fifty K-12 schools founded before 1798 that exist today, seven of which are in Massachusetts, and the many others dating back to this time that have since closed, share a few things in common. They were founded to offer white boys and girls an opportunity, not to resist the government's injustice, and Black youth were not included.

In 1855, the African School joined the list of schools that have since closed. Some fifty years prior to that decision, the public debate surrounding the politics of quality education for Black children reinforced the argument that the African School was first. Independence requires a degree of privatization, which necessitates funding for land, building costs, school equipment, and teachers' salaries. Along with the initial investment from parents, financial support came from notable white ministers, church followers, the Black community overall, and the most significant contributor, Black sailors.[39] Prince Hall is noted as the school's first teacher, but subsequent teachers included members

34

of the African Society and two students from Harvard University. The collaborative efforts of community members seeking independence and wealthy white supporters, some of whom served on the Boston School Committee, enabled the school to find its second home on Belknap Street in 1803 and relocate to the African Meeting House by 1806. In 1812, "the School Committee, undoubtedly impressed with…establishing a separate school, and perhaps eager to exercise control over this autonomous school developing outside the system of public schools, began,…subsidizing separate education in Boston."[40]

It makes little sense to categorize the African School as a private institution. Each petition for public funds addressed the Boston School Committee on *behalf of people of color* and made the claim for Black children at large.[41] Private schools did no such thing. Private is not simply the opposite of public; for much of U.S. educational history, entering a private school required admittance and admission. The African School did no such thing. While the physical capacity at each location was limited, there is no evidence to suggest that interested Black students were ever turned away for being ill-prepared, unable to pay, or certainly not for the color of their skin. In fact, white and Black donors gave generously in the hope that the school would reach more students. More specifically, wealthy businessman Abiel Smith left a sizeable gift to the city upon his death in 1815. His instructions were, "apply the whole income to the maintenance and support of school, or schools, under their direction, for the instruction of people of color, meaning Africans and their descendants either colored or mixed in reading, writing and arithmetic, in such place, places and manner as said selectmen shall deem best."[42] As a consequence of this gift, white politicians elected by a white public had an overwhelming voice in the affairs of the school. Having made no investment themselves, the future of the African School was in the hands of non-Africans.

The new arrangement with the School Committee came after years of support from individual citizens who, while expressing goodwill for the school, did not impose executive direction. Private donations were one thing, but city funding was a Trojan horse. Many in the Black community initially welcomed this support, but soon regretted the intervention and oversight. Between 1820 and 1830, the city's white political leadership, along with the Boston School Committee, seized administrative control of the school, stripping Black families of political agency. "They no longer had control over their school. Instead, it was subject to an indifferent school board, which kept it inferior in terms of building, grounds, appropriations, teacher staffing, supervision, salaries, curriculum, location, and maintenance."[43]

At this point, independence was fully compromised, and the pursuit of quality education shifted to a battle against separate and unequal schooling. Over the years, city officials opened two primary schools and an intermediate school in the cramped Belknap Street area. While they were adding more facilities, the School Committee gutted the heart of the program by removing Black adults from the classroom. Before city control, Black students experienced the care of instructors familiar with their lives. Children born free were schooled with children whose parents were considered fugitives, and all of them received lessons in reading, writing, nationalism, and the condition of Black people in America, Africa, and Haiti. This changed drastically over time. Ignoring widespread complaints and families choosing to stay out of school, the School Committee installed white leadership for twenty straight years and sixty-seven percent of the years overall.[44] Political activism and mounting public pressure eventually forced the city to construct a new building as a half-hearted attempt to provide equality. The endowment left by Abiel Smith, for whom the new school was named, constituted much of the city's support for Black education. No longer called the African School, it would be a stretch to categorize the handful of Black schools, including the newly opened Smith School, as public, private, or independent. They were separate.

This early American experiment with a free Black community foreshadows the types of control, attempts to disgrace, and legal obstacles the descendants of slavery would face to access quality education. For more than forty years, Boston engineered a separate school system for Black and white children, providing a blueprint for segregation throughout the country. Why did school officials corrupt the original intent of Black Bostonians, whose only desire was to be separate from racism? Well, the answer is simple: enough white people wanted to be separate from Black people. And they used the following rule to create legal segregation: "applicants for admission to our schools (with the exception and provision referred to in the preceding rule) are especially entitled to enter the schools nearest to their place of residence. The exception here is for separate schools; that is, colored children."[45] By 1850, a Black parent's challenge to this rule had failed in the courts, and the doctrine of "separate but equal" was born, becoming a legal framework with chilling effects on American life until Brown v. Board of Education defeated it one hundred years later. Black Bostonians, nevertheless, persisted and, with the help of abolitionists and advocates for quality education, forced the state's public schools to desegregate in 1855.

In other parts of the commonwealth, the origin story of school reads quite differently. No explicit mention of race was needed then, and like many of today's independent schools, what's been preserved is completely race-neutral. We have seen how the courts and the general public responded to the request for a single school for Black children. "We now come to an item of our history which every son of Fryeburg may contemplate with just pride." This opening statement in the town's centennial celebration, published in 1864, speaks to the founding of Fryreburg Academy, a private school for the town's brightest students.[46]

If the African School is the first independent school, then we will need different language to describe peer schools of that era. During the colonial period, a private school was understood to be a school set in a private home. A teacher might be retained to instruct students in the home of a family willing to pay for private lessons. Or, as in the case of the first schools of Fryeburg, a teacher would assemble students in their personal home. However, as we've seen, "in the year 1647 a law was passed making the support of schools compulsory, and education universal and free."[47] By 1777, the people of Fryeburg moved in that direction and agreed to apportion funds for organized instruction, and thus began the establishment of a public school system.[48] The argument that all children should receive some education guaranteed, secured, and financed by the government would echo positions held during the Common School Movement of the 1830s, credited to Horace Mann. Setting aside color blindness, public education was widely embraced as a necessity to uphold the desired society, and for many wealthy financiers, it became a deeply held religious undertaking. The founders of Fryeburg Academy knew this, and in 1791, they expressed their desire for a *proper school* — a grammar school — to prepare their *rising youth* for the university with studies in ancient Greek and Latin, and they petitioned for funds from the Massachusetts General Court. They requested rights to unapportioned land, "so that the...seat of a Savage Nation...may henceforth become a seat of knowledge and virtue."[49] The Court responded with a land grant of 12,000 acres, later valued at nearly one million dollars, which provided a financial base for the Academy for generations to come.

Massachusetts is home to hundreds of non-public schools with distinct histories. To make better comparisons, we can organize them by their founding mission, religious affiliation or lack thereof, and governance model. Private schools receive no state funding, and according to the National Association of Independent Schools (NAIS) website, independent schools are non-profit private schools governed by an independent board of trustees. Fryeburg Academy, originally of Massachusetts until 1820 when Maine formed into a state, is worth exploring not because of its categorization today, or because Rev. William Fessenden, whom we have discussed previously, was a lead signature and trustee, but because of its origin. We must learn to read things in color, even when they appear written in black or white. The same court that ignored Prince Hall's plea for a primary school in 1787 approved funding for an advanced school in Fryeburg four years later. The rule — education is a weapon to be controlled for some and gifted to others. The exception occurs only when the gifted make different choices.

Rev. Fessenden's sixth child, Samuel, should stand out for the choices he made, but unfortunately, schools do not teach much about abolition. Samuel attended Fryeburg Academy while Daniel Webster was a teacher and principal. Samuel studied the law under Webster, who once described him as a *young man without many equals.* [50] The admiration was mutual as the two shared similar worldviews and politics. As the years passed, Webster ascended in the political arena and as a trial lawyer before the Supreme Court of the United States. Webster also acted as godfather to Samuel's children, and Samuel's sixth child, Daniel Webster Fessenden, was even named in honor of his dad's mentor. However, by 1850, Samuel was a staunch abolitionist, and U.S. Secretary of State Webster took a public stance on slavery that derailed the lifelong relationship. Embroiled in the controversial compromise between free and slave states, Webster resorted to enforcing the wildly unpopular Fugitive Slave Act as an attempt to preserve the Union. War was on the horizon, and the right to own Black bodies was a political chess piece, but for Samuel, this was a moral red line. Privately, Secretary Webster expressed anti-slavery beliefs that were inconsistent with his pro-slavery politics, and hoping to avoid exposure, Webster wrote to Samuel requesting a return of his letters, which effectively ended their relationship.

Samuel Fessenden held many titles and professions throughout his life, including father, husband, teacher, lawyer, state representative, state senator, major general of the Massachusetts militia, and member of the Congregational Church, which at times led to conflicts. None more so than when he adopted an unwavering stance against the institution of slavery. Political partisanship was intense during this era, and

Samuel was a towering figure. Constituents who applauded his fiscal and religious conservatism denounced his incorruptible enmity for slavery.[51] Common sentiment in the *free* North included sympathy for slave states, the inferiority of Black people, the support of gradual emancipation, African colonization, and preservation of the Union above all. "Long before the anti-slavery agitation, he [Samuel] was an intense anti-slavery man and was inflexibly opposed to that provision in the constitution which gave increased representation to the slave-holding states by counting three-fifths of their slaves."[52]

Samuel Fessenden practiced law and served as a representative from Maine while the state was still part of Massachusetts. By 1818, he also commanded the Twelfth Division of the Massachusetts militia, earning the title of General Fessenden. The 1830s saw the rise of formal abolitionist organizing throughout the region. The Anti-slavery Society of Maine was established with Samuel as the celebrated founder and prominent speaker. Samuel's militant struggle against the evils of slavery was faith-driven. The Congregational Church generally adopted a position of gradual abolition, and many members favored the exportation of free and enslaved Africans back to Africa. To call for the immediate abolition of slavery, equal rights, or citizenship was seen as radical. The *destructionists,* as some called them, were particular irritants that pushed for all three.[53] A few states away, distant cousin Thomas Kendall Fessenden entrenched himself in an abolitionist cause on an international scale. Born in 1813 and an alumnus of Phillips Exeter Academy, Rev. Thomas Kendall Fessenden was a minister in the Congregational Church of Norwich, Connecticut. When a slave ship named La Amistad was directed to New London by the U.S. Navy, the local activists mobilized.

In February 1839, Portuguese slave hunters absconded with dozens of Mende from modern-day Sierra Leone in violation of an 1820 British-Spanish treaty banning the import of African captives. Fifty-three Africans were first transported to Cuba; the Mende men and women were then reloaded aboard the *La Amistad* en route to Caribbean plantations. The Mende revolted, seized control of the ship, and attempted to sail home to Africa, but the surviving crew members, seeking refuge and sympathizers, instead navigated north to the shores of the United States. Whether these Africans, now imprisoned in Connecticut, should be set free, extradited, or meet some other gruesome fate became a matter of international law.[54] Local abolitionists seeking to expose the evils of the slave trade raised awareness and funds for the legal defense. The case galvanized anti-slavery factions throughout the states. Notably, Rev. Thomas Kendall Fessenden's correspondence with New York-based abolitionist Lewis Tappan demonstrates how concerted the movement was growing. Tappan, in the face of pro-slavery threats and rhetoric, published multiple accounts of the trial. Eventually, the captured Africans were proven to be legally free. Tappan's activism, inspired by his revival of faith, was absolutely pivotal. In 1841, Tappan and a handful of others stood on the shores of New York's Staten Island and waved farewell to the Mende as they sailed back across the Atlantic to find home.[55]

In many parts of New England, the antislavery movement continued to gain momentum politically during the 1840s. Samuel Fessenden understood this to mean that he would need to defend his position in the courtroom and on the battlefield. In

1844, his apprentice, Macon Bolling Allen, sought to become the first Black lawyer in U.S. history. Samuel lobbied the court for Allen's admission to the Maine Bar against the desires of political rivals and intolerant white legal minds. Samuel writes in a July 5 letter to his abolitionist partner, Samuel Sewall, "I have the pleasure to inform you that our friend & protege, Mr. Macon B Allen was admitted to practice Law at the Bar of our Distric [sic] Court for this County." He continued, "It was contended that to admit Mr. Allen would disgrace the Bar, no doubt because he was a coloured man...His qualifications were not denied. I think Mr. Allen had the sympathy of a large portion of the people in the court [and] I think quite a number of the jurors wept while I addressed the Court...on the rights of the coloured man, and the wickedness of that prejudice which was crushing him."[56] Samuel closes his letter by updating Sewall on the success of his antislavery tour of the state. While sympathies for the cause of abolition were on the rise, racial bias, and exclusion were the norm of the day. Allen, for example, had a hard time finding clients among the same people who witnessed his matriculation. Despite his credentials and legal acumen, white people could not bring themselves to have a Black man represent them in court. Effectively shut out of practicing law in Maine, Allen moved to Massachusetts and started his own practice.

Popular storytelling of these times will have one believe that a gentleman's squabble over the direction of the Union led to one of the bloodiest wars in American history. The dependence upon slave labor brought about a clinging to institutions and love for individuals who sought to maintain its operation. The other side of this coin was equally true. But some figures hated slavery unquestionably. In 1853, when Northern Democrat Franklin

Pierce was elected President of the United States, Gen. Samuel Fessenden expressed his concern. President Pierce considered abolition a serious threat to the country, and he pledged to enforce the 1850 Fugitive Slave Act. The day after the election, in a conversation with his son, future Senator William Pitt, Gen. Fessenden shared his sense of hopelessness in the struggle for freedom. "Oh, father," said the future politician, "we will renew our fight, and in four years, we will elect our President." In 1856, Gen. Fessenden wrote to another son, Dr. Charles Fessenden, to lament that "the evil genius of our Country has triumphed...I anticipate nothing but evil most dire...the power of the Slave Oligarchy and slavery spread over all the States of the Union." But in 1860, William Pitt's premonition proved true, and the party of the Fessendens nominated and helped elect Abraham Lincoln to the presidency.[57]

Rev. Joseph Palmer Fessenden, born in 1792 in Fryeburg, joined his brother, Gen. Samuel Fessenden, in anti-slavery activism. Rev. Joseph Fessenden is described as never ceasing in his efforts to bring the Congregational Church onto the active anti-slavery platform. Occasionally, Rev. Fessenden would open the Anti-Slavery Society meetings with prayer, and Gen. Fessenden would offer remarks or organize protection for attendees. Across the states, Black abolitionists faced death, torture, and capture. White abolitionists risked personal safety, destruction of property, and the loss of livelihoods and status. If one became too radical, pro-slavery advocates blatantly offered cash rewards for the murder of abolitionists of any background. Gen. Samuel Fessenden was active in the freedom cause for more than twenty-five years until his final days. In 1856, he lived to see the formation of the original Republican Party, centered on the primary issue of slavery. Three of his sons, Senator William Pitt Fessenden, Rep. Samuel Clement Fessenden, and Rep. Thomas A. D. Fessenden, served in the U.S. Congress during the Civil War. Five of Gen. Fessenden's grandsons were officers in the Union Army, one commanding the first integrated battalion. Feeble and blind, Gen. Fessenden lived to hear of the Union Army victory and the end of slavery. He passed in March 1869.

In the same way that Blackness is not a monolith, no collection of anecdotes could ever fully address our question. To answer 'Who are the Fessendens?' is to place limits on some individuals or, at the very least, to invite bias. To answer 'Who are the Fessendens to Black people?' challenges bias in a particular way. The sum total of Black memory taken away from us is incalculable, but despite the lack of completeness, the decision to center Black people in our work is necessary. What results, therefore, will be sufficient.

One of the greatest statements about a Fessenden comes from one of the greatest Black Americans. The iconic abolitionist-orator, Fredrick Douglass, befriended Gen. Fessenden and thanked him in his autobiography.[58] Additionally, Douglass is quoted as saying, "I was at a public anti-slavery meeting at Portland. I began my speech and my words stirred up some opposition from fellows of the baser sort, who undertook to break up my meeting. When the turmoil was at its height, General Fessenden arose, and with his impressive dignity rebuked the turbulence, vindicated the right of speech, and secured order and decorum. He was one of the large brothers of the human race; and I must not omit to say here as my recollection of this good man, that in the early days of anti-slavery, when I was yet newly from the house of bondage, when

45

prejudice against color was rampant, and even took the form of malice, when the mad dog cry of amalgamation affrighted the souls of many, he was brave enough to make me a welcome guest at his fireside."[59]

At the age of 59, Frederick Douglass is pictured front row at the 1877 Reunion for First Maine Cavalry veterans of the Civil War. Douglass was on a speaking tour of New England when he received an invitation to speak before a familiar audience. Frederick Douglass, Old Orchard Beach, 1877. [circa 1877]. Item 6434. Old Orchard Beach, YORK County, ME. Maine State Archives. https://www.mainememory.net/record/6434

CHAPTER 2

marriage, then I give, devise and bequeath said property to the American Missionary Association of the State of New York, in trust nevertheless that the use and income thereof shall be expended by them for the care and maintenance of the Union School of Martin in the State of Florida, for Colored Children, the same to be appropriated and expended under the same terms and conditions as are set forth in deed of land in said Martin, from Frank Laine to said American Missionary Association of New York, except that in case said income shall not, in the judgment of said trustee be needed for the support of said Union School, then said income may be, in the discretion of said trustee, used for scholarships for colored students in any other school or college. III. The land and buildings

Ferdinand Fessenden's will, where he stipulates land to the American Missionary Association for the education of Black children.

T
he night I first read about Fessenden Academy, my family had to endure another session of *you gotta study our own history because they'll never tell you.* By then, they had heard it all. The days of virtual learning placed each of our classrooms within earshot of the living room. They would hear me give talks and participate in countless equity workshops and Africana studies lectures. My wife and I have tried to frame our two children's independent school experience with great intentionality. Beginning at home, our family has journeyed from

a private, racially diverse, Islamic school, to a predominantly white rural public school, to a primarily Black public charter school. At each stop along this journey, some moment forced us to question our decision as parents. We spent equal time helping with homework and helping our children fortify an identity that a school could not break. Now, each of us was at a historically white independent school, and my son was at Fessenden with me. I thought we had seen it all. But there was no simple answer to my son's question, "Why are there two Fessenden schools?"

Young people are good at asking elephant-sized questions of why. *Why do you look like that? Why are you here?* It is one of the few reasons I envy elementary and middle school teaching. Anything out of place, out of context, or a break from routine begets a why. But answering why is rarely as simple as the question itself, let alone sufficient. 'Why?' can be the most unpleasant question, especially if one is not prepared. So we teach young people to ask something softer, more academic, such as 'how?'. We fill books and libraries with answers to these hows — but asking why is balance-seeking and knowing why is wisdom. The answer comes from experience. Give a Black child enough time, and they will tell you why things are as they are. Initially, as I attempted to understand this particular racial paradox and educational juxtaposition, I pursued the logic of how. I needed to know more about this Black parallel to the Fessenden school I knew. And how did it come into being? Was it indeed parallel, or something rightfully askew, existing in its own frame of reference? I needed someone to understand the magnitude of this discovery as I saw it. I needed to hear some wisdom, but it would be weeks before I spoke with anyone from Fessenden Academy to explain the why.

During the winter of 2022, like most schools, we - The Fessenden School - were making our way through the calendar. Board meetings, homecoming events, grades, and student evaluations are non-negotiable. Columbus Day, Halloween, Thanksgiving, and Christmas have given way to Indigenous Peoples' Day, a Fall Festival, and the Winter Season. So, with all this going on, I brought my question to our senior leadership team, still trying to find meaning. "Has anyone heard of the Fessenden Academy in Florida?"

There was silence. I waited for some time, and there was more silence. As a teacher, I have seen this type of silence before. As a math teacher, I know it all too well. Usually, it is indicative of a really poor question or, at times, a really good question. I certainly could have offered a better framing, but admittedly, I was still managing my own inner conflicts. By lunchtime, I must have posed the question to every administrator and colleague with more than twenty years of experience at our school. The most I could elicit from decades upon decades of living memory was two vague recollections: "Every once in a while, someone will call the wrong number looking for Fessenden in Florida," said one colleague. Another remembered finding something about another Fessenden school in the research leading up to the centennial anniversary yearbook, *The Fessenden School, Along Right Lines from the Beginning.* I knew Fessenden Academy existed, and I was thankful that I wasn't alone, but the overall silence sparked more interest. How has this gone overlooked for so many years? My curiosity could not rest. I ended each encounter with, "Did I mention this is a Black Fessenden school, and it is the first Fessenden school?"

It did not take me too long to piece some of the history together: a small community of freedmen opened a school in 1868, by 1900 the Fessenden Academy was a private, coeducation boarding school — one of the best schools in the state, and by 1951 the Academy closed and reopened as a public high school a year later. I had bits of info, but no memory. Eventually, I located the Fessenden Alumni Association via social media and began sending out emails. Days later, I spoke with Fessenden High School alumnus, Mr. Whitfield Jenkins, and then Fessenden Academy graduate, Dr. Gilbert Raiford. Beforehand, I had rehearsed several explanations for calling these gentlemen. These were my elders, and each of them held important details of the Fessenden story. What could I say to introduce myself, and why should these kind folks care? As I wrestled internally, I recalled conversations with my older loved ones. I knew to use my time with them effectively, to ask broad questions, and, most importantly, to listen.

Mr. Jenkins was kind and patient; he pointed me to a half dozen resources and articles online. But I had mountains of questions and needed to pace myself. Mr. Jenkins sensed my passion for discovery and suggested I speak with someone from the Fessenden Academy era. I learned that there were only a few living members from this legacy period when Fessenden was a private school, and Mr. Jenkins recommended Dr. Raiford, whom I contacted. After rambling through an introduction, Dr. Raiford softly responded, "Ah, you're from the Fessenden in the North." I smiled through the phone. Like when two distant relatives discover that their parents were, in fact, cousins, I felt seen. I was proud, not of my affiliation with the Fessenden School, but of their independence from it.

****

From Fort Mose, the first legally established free African settlement in North America, to Eatonville, the oldest incorporated all-Black town in North America, Florida has been a seat of Black independence for centuries. The underbelly of such a prideful legacy is marked by violent repression - including denial, erasure, banning, and silence.

Spanish Florida was considered a sanctuary for many Africans and their descendants for more than one hundred years. Slavery existed within the colony since the 1500s, but with a noteworthy distinction from the British colonies. Spanish law restricted slave labor in Florida from reaching the scale of its already profitable and harsh West Indies sugar plantations. St. Augustine, described as the nation's oldest city, was established in 1565 by Spanish colonists, and Africans, free and enslaved, were among the first to settle and defend the region. In 1687, the first group of reported runaways took refuge in the city. Elsewhere in Florida, runaways, also known as maroons, allied with Indigenous communities to form factions of Black Seminoles. Six years later, Spanish King Charles II decreed legal emancipation for all runaways who converted to Catholicism - he hoped to secure his position in the region and defend the Florida colony from the encroaching English.[60]

Exacerbating tensions between English slaveholders and Spanish colonists, for decades the enslaved populations in Carolina and Georgia continued to make use of the underground railroad that led south to Florida. This led to clashes on the ground and tense imperial diplomacy over land, property, profit, and most certainly slavery. In 1733, the Spanish crown reinforced its decree, stipulating that English slaveholders would receive no reimbursement for lost slaves, and runaways would be granted freedom after four years of service to the crown. Nearing one hundred families, the free Black community of St. Augustine grew so significantly that by 1738, members were granted an area called Garcia Real de Santa Teresa de Mose, or Fort Mose. Fort Mose became a community of skilled masons, carpenters, ironsmiths, builders, teachers, and warriors.[61]

Before the Revolutionary War, the English highly regarded the land in East Florida for its grain yield, and mid-Florida was known to be fertile and ripe for cotton production, but eliminating sanctuary in Florida was a priority for the soon-to-be United States. As skirmishes carried on between the Spanish Florida militia and South Carolinian and Georgian slaveholders, the royals of Spain and Great Britain remained at odds. The threat to freedom was particularly felt by Black and Indigenous peoples. Service in the Florida militia was a pathway to emancipation and a welcome alternative to re-enslavement. In 1740, as fighting intensified, Fort Mose was captured and subsequently destroyed. A decade later, the Black community rebuilt its settlement, housing sixty-seven families. Eventually, by treaty, Florida would fall under English control. In response, the Black community of Fort Mose completely abandoned their homes in favor of Havana, Cuba. For the estimated thousands of free and enslaved Black Floridians who remained, Secretary of State Thomas Jefferson pressed for the end of religious sanctuary in Florida. And, with the passing of the Fugitive Slave Act of 1793 and the acquisition of Florida as a U.S. territory in 1821, the response to Black independence was clear: a return to enslavement.[62]

Tens of millions of dollars were spent, and countless lives were lost to remove the Indigenous tribes from Florida. Certainly, this is an important topic worthy of further review. As it applies to our story, this violent purging allowed wealthy slaveholders and aspiring capitalists to venture further south into Florida to extract more labor. Advertisements for land and profit spurred a cotton rush from slave-holding planters in the surrounding Southern states. The message was clear: if one could handle the trek and owned enough slave labor, a fortune could be made. A steady stream of settlers moving to Florida increased the population from 34,730 to 54,477 between 1830 and 1840; almost half of them were enslaved. [63] John Marshall Martin, born in 1832 in South Carolina, was one such individual. The Martin family came to Virginia around 1690 and, within two generations, became well-established among the planter class of South Carolina.[64]

During the 1840s, the political will for Florida statehood aligned with the territory's dependence on chattel slavery. The Second Seminole War (1835-1842) was in the rearview, and more white Southerners were settling deeper into Florida. Violence and brutality cleared the land to maximize crop production, and violence and brutality would continue. At the time, U.S. policy required that any free state joining the union must be balanced by an additional slave state. When Congress approved the Iowa-Florida Act of 1845, Florida became the 27th state and Iowa the 29th. With its political power established, Florida had even more opportunities to offer. For John Martin, after graduating from military school, these were the conditions facilitating his foray into Florida's Marion County in 1855.

Florida's initial statehood was short-lived. Within months of Abraham Lincoln's election to the presidency in November 1860, South Carolina, Mississippi, and Florida were the first states to secede from the Union. The impetus - *preserving a southern way of life* - was rooted in a fight over the *right* to enslave Black bodies for profit and political power. At the time, John Martin owned three thousand acres of land and fifty-three enslaved persons.[65] Many of Martin's career accolades proudly appear on his gravestone. In 1861, he volunteered and emerged as Captain of the Marion Light Artillery. But after suffering an injury, Martin left the battlefield. In 1862, he served as Florida's representative for the First Confederate Congress — a position that brought distinction (at the time of his death in 1921, Martin was the lone surviving member of that radical body). Preferring armed combat to politics, Martin declined reelection and instead rejoined his troops, earning the rank of Colonel for Florida's Ninth Infantry. A veteran of war and commander in several pivotal battles, Col. Martin served under Confederate General Robert E. Lee in 1865. On April 9 of that year, in Appomattox, Virginia, both men and their army surrendered to Union troops, essentially ending the violent and brutal Civil War.

Only a month prior to that surrender, *a justifiable source of pride* and an example of Black independence occurred in Marion County. I came to learn of this story during a visit with Fessenden Academy alumnus Dr. Raiford in the summer of 2023, when he gifted me Bruce Seaman's *To Succeed Where Others Failed*. I'll recount the tale as he told it to me, fit for the big screen: as the Civil War drew to a close, thirty troops under Black command undertook a daring raid of a key sugar plantation in hostile territory. In March of 1865, from the Union base camp in

Jacksonville, Florida, Sergeant-Major Henry James of Lancaster, Pennsylvania, a free Black man, convinced his commanders to embark on a risky mission that would take soldiers one hundred miles into the heart of Confederate Florida. Sixteen free men from Philadelphia's 3rd U.S. Colored Infantry (3rd USCT) and six formerly enslaved men from South Carolina's 34th U.S. Colored Troops (34th USCT) unit agreed to risk their lives, along with seven Black civilians and one lone white soldier from the 107th Ohio Volunteer Infantry. Traveling clandestinely by river and land to Marion County, the team of thirty attacked the plantation of Col. Jehu F. Marshall and freed a reported ninety-five people from slavery. In their attempt to raid another plantation and free others, the team suffered casualties. Now traveling eighty miles on foot with a caravan of freedmen and captured goods, the troops barely eluded capture from the Confederate Cavalry as they entered the gates of St. Augustine on March 12, 1865.[66] One of the final scenes of the War and the only battle to take place in Marion County, this important history is the type of memory often overlooked by many academics and kept out of classrooms today. Had it not been for Dr. Raiford, whom I interviewed several times over the period of my research, the lesson would have missed me as well — memory is far greater than a collection of facts.

Days after speaking with Dr. Raiford, I reached out to Linda Ward, whose family has lived around Martin, Florida, for several generations. We met during my first visit to Fessenden Elementary School in 2023, and I was excited to learn more about her family's narrative. Ms. Ward connected me with her relative and family historian, Larry Rose, and surprisingly, the name of Captain Dickison came up. I was familiar with this name from my conversation with Dr. Raiford, so the coincidence had instant meaning. The Confederate Cavalry that chased the Black troops during their mission belonged to the 2nd Florida Infantry, commanded by Captain J. J. Dickison. Previously, Capt. Dickison served under Col. Martin, and he was also a South Carolinian slaveholder who had settled in Florida. In 1865, as the Confederate Army was losing ground and momentum in areas such as Virginia, Captain Dickison and his Confederate forces were nonetheless outmaneuvering the Union Army in key parts of Florida. Capt. Dickison was beloved locally and known militarily for guerrilla-like war tactics, raiding Union lines, and protecting the interior of Florida.[67] Black troops from the 54th Massachusetts Regiment, 34th USCT, and 3rd USCT, under white Union command, fought Dickison's men and were aware of his pursuits. In this context, the Marshall Plantation Raid, executed by a Black squadron and planned by a Black commander, gives meaning to the remark and title of Seaman's book, *To Succeed Where Others Failed*. Indeed, above all else in U.S. history, how the Civil War is remembered today is rooted in what we take pride in.

The Christian Recorder was the official newspaper of the African Methodist Episcopal Church. As one of the oldest existing periodicals published by Black Americans, I wasn't surprised to learn the Marshall Plantation Raid was first documented here. During the Civil War and the era of Reconstruction, *The Christian Recorder* shared news about the church and regional politics that affected Black people. On April 22, 1865, the paper published a letter from the 3rd USCT Sgt. Henry S. Herman entitled "The Jacksonville Expedition." In it, he summarizes, "This expedition reflects great credit on Sergeant Major James, for the masterly manner in which it was commanded, and gives further proof that a colored man with proper training can command among his fellows and succeed where others have failed."[68] The others here are the white Union commanders who often took a paternalistic and dismissive approach with Black troops. Sgt. Herman signs his letter, "I am still an ardent lover of my race and a soldier."

The lives of Black people in the Confederate States were constantly changing during the war. The financial price of rebellion fell to wealthy slaveowners, who needed to secure their human property and squeeze their labor even tighter. Union-led plantation attacks freed as many as possible, and others brazenly fled captivity to take up arms against the slaveholding regime. In response, many enslaved persons were moved further south to avoid emancipation by revolt or war, and others were pushed into slave impressment — a military policy that allowed commanders to seize property and material for the war. "The government of the Confederate States faced shortages of all kinds…and used slaves for military-related tasks." Assignments included fortifying strategic positions, digging entrenchments, and building obstructions, and despite it being called a *slave payroll*, the contract was with the owner.[69] There is no record of a unit of Black troops fighting for the Confederacy; logic and Southern racist pride tell us that. Yet, under inconceivable duress, some enslaved Black people aided the Confederate army. Much like the enslaved persons on the Marshall plantation whose labor supplied the Confederacy, slaveholders could task individuals with work near the front lines. The 2nd Florida Cavalry consisted of horsemen, and care for the animals and carriages fell to enslaved teamsters. On March 20, 1865, eight days after losing the chase of Black troops on the Jacksonville Expedition, Capt. Dickison surrendered to Union forces. This surrender emancipated Thomas B. Ward, a teamster and ancestor of Linda Ward and Larry Rose.[70]

The Confederate defeat in 1865 brought turmoil and ruin to many slaveholders. Wealthier families would recover in time, but for most Southern fighters - those lacking formal education and property - there would be no compensation for their socioeconomic and emotional ruin and loss. Across the South, an agonizing shame and resentment shared the air with a collective exhale from the recently emancipated. These freedmen grappled with an unparalleled hierarchy of needs and direct, hate-filled opposition. Many sought to locate loved ones, repair families, secure resources, and achieve literacy for themselves and their offspring. By 1868, a community of Black families residing on the land owned by Col. Martin aspired to build a school. Among the group were war veterans and many who would have known the Martin plantation intimately. If naming their school carried a sense of pride or sought to create memory, few names could've been more overt than the Union School. And, certainly, for Thomas Ward, this was not coincidental.

The Black residents of Marion County share oral traditions that describe Col. Martin as an uncommon slaveholder. One account claims Col. Martin never used white overseers like many planter-class peers. It is difficult to read much into this report because utilizing a Black overseer instead of compensating a white overseer could have been a cost-saving approach. Additionally, an overseer's race does not preclude the use of the most inhumane tactics. However, Col. Martin is also credited for encouraging literacy. On the Martin plantation, an enslaved person who sought reading skills faced no punishment. To say the least, this would have been unconventional for the time. Additionally, and perhaps why records are hard to verify, scrutiny from other slaveholders could have jeopardized Col. Martin's standing. Ultimately, the precursor to the Union School included a rich sentiment towards education and Black self-determination. Unique to this community in Florida, however, was the presence of literate Black adults and their desire to teach succeeding generations.

Located in Martin, Florida, the Union School began in a modest log cabin built by the community and financed by Thomas B. Ward. Father Ward, as he was later called, was a fair-skinned Black man. His father, William Ward, was the slaveholder of his mother, Louisa. Originally from Greensville, South Carolina, Ward returned home after his emancipation from the Confederacy. Upon rejoining his family, he negotiated a labor contract in South Carolina. Sometime before 1868, Ward and his family migrated to Marion County and found work near the future school. Father Ward established the Union School and the Union Church in the same vicinity. Similar schools across the South were open to both children and adults, serving as a central anchor for the community. Families would often sacrifice whatever they could to pay for lessons; however, a child was rarely turned away. Some of the first teachers at the Union School were white women from Northern states. In 1877, the first Black teacher arrived, and by 1890, the school reportedly enrolled seventy-five pupils. We do not have many records from this early period, but Chapter Five will take a closer look at the school's founding and the transition of leadership between 1868 and 1951.

To appreciate the legacy of the Union School, it is worth examining the national and statewide approach to education.

During the nineteenth century, when legal slavery was still practiced and public education was not yet widespread, schools were generally accessible only to those who could afford them. Following the Revolutionary War, the federal government determined that a portion — one square mile or 640 acres — per town of newly controlled lands would be set aside for public education. The center-most section of land was intended for sale, or the benefit of schools for every child.[71] This principle, attributed to Thomas Jefferson, was recodified in a 1787 law requiring new states to encourage *schools and the means of education* for each town.[72] By 1802, Ohio was the first state formed from a territory to receive federal land grants for public education. Decades later, in 1830, a U.S House of Representatives report entitled *Land for Education* noted, "Congress has granted one entire section...in all the States upon the national territory...to be enjoyed forever by the inhabitants of such township, for the use of schools."[73] In Florida, where land was acquired from Spain and the removal of sovereign indigenous nations, this meant a federal investment in public education for white children preceded statehood.

Horace Mann is credited with founding the Common School movement of the 1830s; however, his hope that public dollars could fund schools in every community was not a novel idea. Prince Hall and Boston's Black community articulated this position in 1787, almost a decade before Mann's birth and at the same time as future President Thomas Jefferson. By 1860, Florida had fifty-two common schools and fourteen academies. Many of the academies were private Christian seminaries. Other private schools resembled the home model discussed previously. A wealthy slaveholder would arrange for a teacher to teach inside the home and share the cost with neighboring families.[74] For white Floridians lacking resources, such as small farmers, plantation workers, or skilled laborers, access to public education was not a top priority. In fact, at the state level, there was a divestment in public education. Before the Civil War, the federal government granted Florida 908,503 acres of land for common schools.[75] As is the case today, education fell under the state's jurisdiction, and proceeds from land sales were allocated to other internal improvements.

Researcher and professor of education, Thomas E. Cochran, explains that the "widespread indifference" toward education among white Floridians before the Civil War, "is evident by the fact that the people were unwilling to provide funds for the proper support of schools, and second, that they also failed to see that their children attend." According to Florida's Superintendent of Schools, sentiments improved from general *apathy* to an *awakening interest* in common schools by 1860. Notably, Black children were still without rights. Yet, while the war effort devastated many facilities and drained public funds for schools, it was the "fear that coeducation of races would be forced upon them" that led to a divestment of will.[76] Consequently, the development of public schools, namely for white children, was delayed for another decade.

Historian and professor of education, James Anderson, opens his seminal book, *The Education of Blacks in South 1860-1935,* with the following analysis:

Blacks emerged from slavery with a strong belief in the desirability of learning to read and write. This belief was expressed in the pride with which they talked of other ex-slaves who learned to read and write in slavery and in the esteem in which they held literate blacks. It was expressed in the intensity and frequency of their anger at slavery for keeping them illiterate. "There is one sin that slavery committed against me," professed one ex-slave, "which I will never forgive. It robbed me of my education." The former slaves' fundamental belief in the value of literate culture was expressed most clearly in their efforts to secure schooling for themselves and their children.

Black efforts for educational access did not happen in a vacuum. In the aftermath of the Civil War, reconstructing the country was the national priority. The insurgent states were in political limbo, and Union troops remained stationed throughout the South. In December of 1865, Sen. William Pitt Fessenden from Maine and Sen. Thaddeus Stevens of Pennsylvania served as chairmen of the Joint Committee on Reconstruction. The committee debated the grounds on which the eleven rebellious states would rejoin the federal government. For the political elite, even though Black individuals, including war veterans, the previously free, and the newly emancipated had served the Union, there was little consideration for what was to happen now that the end was achieved.

Sen. Fessenden's son, Francis Fessenden, documented his father's thoughts on reconstruction: "The millions of colored people were thrown without protection upon the charities of the world in hostile communities angered at the freedom of their slaves. They were so freed because the country was compelled to avail itself of their services, as well as to deprive their masters of the material aid they furnished them in contest against the Union." In acknowledging the service of Black soldiers, Fessenden remarks, "the country could carry on a great war, but the moment the clash of arms had ceased it became powerless to provide for the necessary results of that war."[77] Many of the necessities Fessenden alludes to fell under the purview of the Freedmen's Bureau. Established before the end of the war, the Bureau encountered intense political resistance during Reconstruction that derailed its ambitions. Few could understand the Freedmen's Bureau as a moral, justice-serving means of repair. Instead, Southern white grievance eclipsed the bureau's work. Along with mismanagement, widespread outcry claimed the Bureau and Congress *were taxing white people to support the blacks*, while leaving freedmen relatively alone.

Black communities and their allies made headway in the space left vacant by the federal government. Localized small investments from Black families and philanthropic organizations provided the early schoolhouses with their financial start, but fundraising was just one of many needs. Finding teachers was another hurdle. In all, Florida had nearly thirty Black schools in operation by 1865, and more than half of them were taught by freed persons who achieved literacy while enslaved. The remaining teachers were usually from Northern states, some of whom braved the journey south during the war. It was clear by 1866 that Florida wanted to wash its hands of funding and staffing Black schools. The state legislature even attempted to tax *all males of color between the ages of 21 and 45* years to subsidize the few schools that existed.[78] By 1868, the supply of Northern teachers traveling into the Deep South increased. Abolitionist organizations and missionaries sponsored the salaries for many of these educators. Others volunteered to teach without pay, and many of them were white women from affluent families. However, the work of Black teachers, administrators, and members of the American Missionary Association (AMA) was significant, expanding, and a key ingredient for our story. As Clara M. DeBoer highlights in *His Truth is Marching On*, "In 1867, almost one-third of all the teachers reported by the Freedmen's Bureau at work in the South were commissioned by the AMA."

Founded in 1846, the AMA was comprised mainly of Congregationalists and Presbyterians who believed sincerely in abolition. Lewis Tappan was a founding member and served as treasurer and spokesperson. "Although it…was not primarily an educational organization, it (the AMA) did more to educate the freed slaves than any other organization, including the Freedmen's Bureau," writes DeBoer. At times, AMA teachers pushed beyond the Union Army's front lines. AMA missionaries would offer clothing to the women and children of enlisted Black soldiers. Two hundred and fifty AMA missionaries and teachers were living among the freedmen by 1865.[79]

The first AMA teacher on record as working and living in Florida is Carrie Jocelyn of Brooklyn, New York. A Congregationalist Church member with family roots in abolition and early Black suffrage, Jocelyn taught Union soldiers at St. Augustine. By the end of the war, the AMA established schools in Gainesville, Jacksonville, Key West, Magnolia, Monticello, Ocala, St. Augustine, Strawberry Mills, and Tallahassee. White Floridians did not openly welcome these northern white educators. Teachers could anticipate anything from refusal of lodging to attempted murder. "They were insulted, sneered at, and occasionally, threatened by white mobs." In general, the white opposition was less about the education of the freedmen and more about the type of education the freedmen received.[80]

Some of the earliest lessons taught during this period included learning arithmetic, writing, and reading Biblical passages. The dignity and pride that came with literacy were not bound to age. Teachers reported having students who were well into the latter stages of their lives. Schoolhouses operated throughout the day to accommodate the community's desire for education and the demand for their labor. In a 1971 volume of *The Journal of Negro Education*, Joe Richardson cites an 1865 letter in which an AMA official wrote, "One man, who claimed to be ninety-five, attended evening classes regularly after working all day." Here, we see a foreshadowing of a timeless tension between the services of the Black body and the development of the Black mind. Time has certainly added layers of nuance, but labor can easily circumscribe a people without memory. The U.S. government and most of its citizenry have considered people of African descent as a commodity or a liability, with little thought as to what lies between these extremes.

AMA teachers, Black and white, understood the need to develop self-pride via education. As Richardson writes:

The former slave was encouraged to discard all practices that reminded him of slavery, including tipping the hat and giving the inside of the sidewalk to white men. What the teachers considered indications of manhood and dignity, southern whites considered insolence. Lectures were sometimes given on the glories of early Africa. Textbooks contained antislavery poems and material which presented the South unfavorably. A widely used reader, *The Freedmen's Book*, edited by L. Maria Child, was dedicated to Negro Civil War hero Robert Smalls. Among the readings included were: a eulogy of the Haitian revolutionary, Toussaint L'Ouverture; the story of the slave mutiny of the brig

Creole; John Brown's exploits at Harpers Ferry; several antislavery poems by Whittier; an abolition speech by William Lloyd Garrison; and the story of Ignatius Sancho, a Spanish Negro who achieved some distinction in letters in Eighteenth Century Europe. AMA teachers were not content to teach just reading and writing. They were determined to construct a new democratic society.

For the AMA, teacher placement was absolutely race-conscious. As early as 1870, the AMA publication *The American Missionary* advertised and emphasized the urgent need for Black teachers in southern schools. Rural locations were especially challenging assignments for any teacher. However, when possible, the organization recognized that Black communities stood to benefit psychologically from seeing representations of themselves in front of the classroom. Support for these endeavors came in the form of fundraising and volunteering, but classroom teaching was the clear frontline. As the Reconstruction years drew to a close, promoting Black teachers went from a preference to a necessity. Southern whites desired for the races to remain separate and would enforce these norms with violence. Initially, the aim was to prolong the effect of centuries of degradation, slow Black progress, and halt Northern intervention. In time, as Black professionals emerged from universities and trained Black teachers entered the classroom, segregation became law. Black teachers, even today, speak of their duty to serve, mentor, and educate Black children rather than simply to teach. This was certainly true in an era when careers were closed to many, and the need for affirming instruction was dire. The AMA, by consequence, helped to establish a legacy and a pipeline of teachers from Black Colleges to Black common schools.

Clara DeBoer writes, "Although W.E.B. Dubois and Booker T. Washington disagreed about many things, they were one in their praise of the AMA....These two men, giants among Black Americans and so different in their approaches to the struggles for equality, were effusive in their praise of AMA teachers. Washington called what they did *one of the most thrilling parts* of our history, and Dubois said unequivocally it was "the finest thing in American history." One way to capture the magnitude of the AMA's impact is to consider the legacies of Atlanta University, Berea College, Dillard College, Fisk University, Hampton University, Howard University, and many others — all associated with the AMA.

Many great Black institutions carry non-African names as the imprint of imperialism, racism, and class. In Florida, Fessenden, as an example, has a legacy centered on Black Pride and achievement. Decades of toil, triumph, and joy have engendered generations of Black people in Marion County and beyond to a name and a purpose. As for the name, it originates with Ferdinand Stone Fessenden, born in Boston in 1838. A distant cousin to the abolitionist Samuel Fessenden of Maine, Ferdinand is four generations removed from the first Fessendens born in America. He moved to Florida in 1890, where he encountered a community of striving learners and educators. The meager conditions of the Union School struck such a cord with Ferdinand that he lived out the final chapter of his life in proximity and in support of the burgeoning Academy.

It is hard to enumerate the many challenges that Black schools faced during this era. Economically, demand outpaced the supply of classrooms and teachers statewide; no federal land grants were left for Black common schools, the state's racism closed that door for funding, and a fee-based model excluded far too many. The Union Academy in Gainesville, Florida, established in 1867, and the Howard Academy in Ocala, established in 1866, are peer institutions to the Union School in Martin, Florida. A combination of Freedmen's Bureau support and Northern philanthropy served as a launchpad for their independent start, but eventually, both Union and Howard Academy were absorbed by their respective counties as segregated public schools. Before they transitioned to being state-funded, private dollars available to Florida's Black schools were diverted elsewhere. For example, the Peabody Fund, named after New England-born George Peabody, is said to have shaped educational practices throughout the South from Reconstruction until the 1960s. While the spirit of the nearly two-million-dollar fund was intended to benefit the *entire population* — school-age children of all races — by 1880, only 6.5 percent of the fund went to Black schools.[81]

George Peabody selected the fund's board members, including a personal friend and former Massachusetts Senator Robert Winthrop, as chairman. Among the Trustees were several Confederate loyalists. Further allaying the fears of many Southern elites, Robert E. Lee visited Peabody in August of 1869 and agreed on its utility. The Fund's general agent, former Massachusetts Superintendent and former President of Brown University, Barnas Sears, enacted policies that favored white children and opposed mixed schools. In Florida, Sears intended to build a statewide public educational system. One such policy redirected Peabody funds for use in locations serving at least one hundred white children. Whereas literacy rates still favored white Floridians, Sears reasoned that in many counties, Black schools were already established, and therefore the white population remained in greatest need and presented the best opportunity for usefulness.[82] Despite his religious belief in equality, Sears ultimately administered private funds to some of the most racist public officials in the South. This defunding of public Black and integrated schools sponsored, in part, by wealthy New Englanders, provides more context for the remarkable story of the Union School in Martin, Florida.

Ferdinand Stone Fessenden was not an educator, not in the traditional sense. According to at least one AMA report, Ferdinand favored Episcopal teaching over the more active missionary work led by Congregationalists. The Fessenden family record states, "He was an honest merchant and, in time, was able to open a large store that supplied the Boston and Maine Railroads. He acquired a thorough education and became very proficient in music. He traveled west and later to Florida, where he lived for many years." It was most likely advice from his physician to escape the harsh winters of Boston that brought Ferdinand to Florida, where he encountered the Union School while touring the area. Finding the overcrowded and poorly equipped schoolhouse was a moving experience. Ferdinand then set out to construct a worthy facility for learning and became the primary fundraiser and benefactor.

In 1897, AMA Secretary August F. Beard remarked that of Florida's 2051 school buildings, only 7 were brick, only 422 had imported furniture, and only 450 were made of undamaged lumber. In this same report, Beard remarks that Fessenden had erected a new building and furnished it with desks, maps, charts, and all necessary equipment for instruction. "A beautiful two-story building with four elegant, airy recitation rooms." The Fessenden family record continues:

He placed quotations from the words of the great thinkers of humanity and pictures of such inspiring spirits as Washington, Lincoln, Webster, Shakespeare, Franklin, Whittier, Longfellow and Mrs. Stowe on the walls. He bought ten acres of land adjacent to the school building and donated it for the campus. Next, he gave the school a small library…and kept the reading room filled with the best literature published. He taught patriotism and emphasized the lesson with a mammoth United States flag. Two organs were next given, and he fitted the school chapel with four hundred chairs, a modern stage, ample dressing rooms, and other facilities.[83]

In Beard's report, he noted that the Union School teachers had received their education from colleges supported by the Association and that the current principal was a graduate of Fisk University. The following passage reveals some of the culturally affirming education students received while benefiting from the relatively superior physical plant.

On a recent occasion when the County Superintendent visited this school, the pupils were gathered in the assembly room to be addressed by him. Noticing upon the walls two large engravings, one of Washington and one of Lincoln, he said, "Children, these are fine pictures, but there should be a picture of your greatest benefactor, one who has done more for you than Washington or Lincoln," having in his mind the generous benefactor of this school. "Children, you all know whom I mean; tell me his name."

The chorus of voices in one accord exclaimed "John Brown," while the Superintendent caught his breath. [84]

Certainly, a scene worth recording, but imagine if the students had shouted Harriet Tubman, Toussaint L'Ouverture, Martin Delaney, Frederick Douglass, or even their principal, one Joseph Wiley.

In the twilight of life, Ferdinand came to understand the gravity of his calling and the powerful forces working against him. Wiley writes, "Never before had he been so deeply interested in the welfare of the poor, but now it seemed that a new vision of duty dawned upon him. In the face of criticism and many forms of discouragement, he, without superabundant means, built a two-story school building. He fitted it with maps and the best modern school furniture." Even a large, finely tuned organ was acquired, but Ferdinand knew a sustainable model was critical for the school's survival. He lobbied for financial support from friends in Boston and purchased the adjoining orange grove, hoping to generate future income for the school. Ferdinand's most consequential decision, however, was to partner with the AMA.[85]

Teachers remained the most treasured resource, and recruitment, placement, and compensation were unique challenges during this time. It is believed that Ferdinand met with the leadership of the Union School and proposed a formal alliance with the AMA. At the time, many prominent Black educators had affiliations with universities, schools, and officials supported by the AMA. This alliance made sense for all parties – the school would have access to a pipeline of teachers, Ferdinand could trust the school would continue, and missionary work would now come to this area of Florida. Additionally, the AMA offered a buffer against the interference of the local segregationist school board. By the mid-1890s, the school was deeded to the AMA and years later became known to many as Fessenden Academy. However modest, Ferdinand refused personal recognition during his lifetime and only knew or spoke of the Union School, the original name.

After several attempts to place teachers, in 1898 Secretary Beard selected Joseph Wiley to be the principal of the Union School. A native Tennessean, Wiley attended public school as a child. By 1893, he graduated from Fisk University, earning a classics degree and serving as chief editor of the school newspaper, class historian, and commencement speaker. A brilliant and charismatic leader, Wiley taught at local schools while studying to be a lawyer. In 1896, Wiley earned admission to the Tennessee Bar.[86] Convinced that his religious calling was for the classroom, Wiley and his wife, Josephine, accepted the commission in Florida and set the Union School on a trajectory of excellence. In 1904, Wiley described the years that preceded his arrival: "Was there a set of black boys or girls made more happy than were those who marched from the dilapidated cabin into this school edifice fifteen years ago? But the good philanthropist had a problem at once. Nice looking and well-furnished schoolhouses are desirable and educative, but teachers to conduct schools that can match such houses are hard to find down this way, and they cost money when they are found...Mr. Fessenden heard of the American Missionary Association, though he knew little about it. He found out, however, and invited Dr. Beard...to come and look...and, if possible, to take management of the school."

As Ferdinand's health wavered, Wiley continued to grow the school's enrollment, physical plant, and curriculum. In May of 1899, Ferdinand is said to have called the senior class to his bedside, where he advised them, "Always seek an education."[87] In his final moments, Ferdinand prayed for the school and for successors to continue his work. His desire was for the academy to remain a center for Black education. Wiley recalled this from his brief time with Ferdinand: "If poor teachers, poor equipment, and poor children yield poor results in the schoolroom, then get better teachers, better equipment that it may be possible for poor children to get better results."[88] Ferdinand was buried near campus, and in 1900, with the support of many community members, the AMA officially renamed the Union School the Fessenden Academy and Industrial School.

Wiley was a diplomat of the highest order. From the AMA's headquarters in New York, Fessenden Academy was its most remote school. Wiley, therefore, operated with discretion, balancing demands from the Association's home office and the aspirations, low and high, of both the local Black and white communities. To be young, gifted, and Black meant cultivating pride amidst degradation and displaying it with precaution. Beyond this, Wiley was wise in modeling how to disarm whites who considered Black education inferior while teaching young Black people to stand tall. Farming was the region's economic base, and Wiley had to earn the confidence of Black parents before he could teach their children. He also had to present a non-threatening school to white leaders concerned with maintaining social norms and curbing challenges to the labor force. Fessenden's industrial program did just that by instituting a ten-grade academic program, which surpassed most in the state.

What was often called a "functional education" appealed to the need for skilled labor and the dreams of future teachers, lawyers, accountants, and politicians.

Wiley and his team of Black teachers developed a program that emphasized moral uplift, Christian-centered ethics, and community. By 1903, Fessenden Academy was the only local school to offer a tenth-grade level of study. Serving more than two hundred and fifty students, the faculty lived on campus, and at least fifty boarding students stayed with local families. For the promise of a Fessenden education, most families sacrificed to make their tuition payments. Wiley advertised the need for general support of the Academy and, more specifically, his desire to erect student dormitories within the pages of *The American Missionary*. Campus expansion mirrored Fessenden's quickly developing teacher pipeline. Among the first tenth-grade graduating class were five young women who passed the state's teacher assessment. The school's reputation was strong, and families outside of Marion County began to take notice. So, too, did the AMA. Wiley's fundraising prowess earned the school gifts from across the political spectrum. The national Congregational stronghold was the most consistent donor, but support from the state level, the Peabody Fund, and a signature award from the Carnegie Fund highlight the universal success of the Fessenden Academy. [89]

Remarkably, Wiley advanced the Academy's facilities and purchased additional land without placing more financial strain on the AMA. Still, his fundraising attempts and campus development drew ire from AMA officials seeking more oversight. Unconventionally, Wiley would use his personal wealth at times to pay school bills, which were reasonably priced because much of the school's upkeep was community-rooted. The overall maintenance of a boarding school provided hands-on learning and employment opportunities. Mitigating some of the cost, Black artisans and local craftsmen joined students to complete building projects. Additionally, service to others was a recurring theme of both religious and racial significance from the beginning of Wiley's tenure. "The object of this school is to train the young of the Negro race to be useful and intelligent Christian citizens."[90] Every student was required to have a Bible, and a prayer service was mandatory. In 1906, Fessenden students demonstrated those lessons with a meaningful donation to the AMA and other relief organizations. Their contribution was acknowledged with the following statement in the national magazine: "Can any other school of three hundred pupils show a better record of self-denial and benevolence?[91]

The Wileys, as a husband-and-wife team, were so successful in their leadership of the Academy that local doubts about the value of Black education and the need for a boarding school soon gave way to praise. Joe Richardson writes that in December of 1908, members of the Marion County Board of Public Instruction visited Fessenden at Wiley's invitation and found it "in the most excellent condition and doing splendid work." The board commended Principal Wiley "for his untiring work and splendid success" and enthusiastically recommended Fessenden to Florida's black students. The Board further stated that "in its opinion, it was the best colored school" in the state. By 1910, the school employed a staff of eleven educators, enrolled more than 300 students, and housed 45 students as boarders. Six of the teachers were college graduates. Fessenden added a four-year normal course from which sixteen men and women graduated as teachers. Many others who had not received diplomas were also teaching in county schools. By 1912, at least a thousand students had attended the school.

Beyond the Academy, Wiley was a staple in the community. He was so well-respected across color lines that his fair skin may have led some to assume he was not Black. Yet, anyone close to him would have discovered he was indeed a race man. Richardson continues, "Although Wiley was overburdened as principal, teacher, business manager, and farm supervisor, he did not neglect the community. He constantly spoke at churches, schools, and farm conventions. He led the fight against legal liquor in his precinct, worked for better public schools, and joined with Ocala Black businessmen in creating the Metropolitan Savings Bank with a capital stock of $25,000 in 1913." Wiley went on to serve as the bank's vice president.

Remarkably, within one generation of slavery, Black self-determination had begun to manifest. Residents in the areas surrounding Fessenden Academy were politically active; they collaborated on farming techniques, banking, and certainly education. No longer collectively destitute and abandoned, examples of excellence were becoming common and often reflected the values established by the dominant class. Undoubtedly, progressive and even radical-minded whites could only imagine Black freedom on their terms and measured by their standards. Perhaps no better example of this exists outside of the church and school. Christian missionary work, at its core, whether internalized as such or rejected, is white saviorism, a direct derivative of white supremacy. Still, the ideals of a meaningful life taught to Fessenden students were unquestionably admirable. Furthermore, for children living with and learning from adults born into bondage, witnessing their autonomy was a special form of dignity. Beyond Fessenden, those young people encountered an unsafe world, and school was their refuge.

To prove self-worth is labor—endless, thankless, traumatizing labor. For Wiley and the Fessenden teachers, successfully instructing Black children also meant disproving racist rhetoric. In a 1909 report to the AMA, Wiley remarked: "Surely the Negros in America should strive earnestly to prove to the world his wisdom that they are a more valuable asset in every way, incommensurably greater than they could be as driven slaves." The Academy celebrated President Lincoln's birthday with songs and orations on this occasion. Wiley continued, "The exchange of vice for virtue, the cabin for the cottage, poverty for property, ignorance for intelligence, and the full development of strong racial characteristics that live on the heights of integrity and industry will continue to show that the children of the former slaves, freed by Lincoln are worthy of his deeds and all they cost."

For readers of *The American Missionary*, Wiley's language appealed to their worldview. Black suffrage, religious conversion, and the teaching of democracy resonated throughout the AMA stronghold. This is evident by the many donations of all sizes that continued to arrive for specific Fessenden initiatives. Fessenden had earned quite a reputation, and signs of student thriftiness, reciprocity in giving, and *Christian character* stood in parallel with prize-winning at state fairs. Indeed, the charitable gifts the AMA received from Black residents near the Academy and from Fessenden students were as impressive as reports of student achievement in the classroom.[92] Wiley's final report includes an ode to Ferdinand at a Christmas celebration and a summary of 1914 standout graduates:

Thirteen years ago for example, little "Mamie" entered here, and this year when she graduated her essay was strong, elegantly expressed and delivered with genuine eloquence. Her subject was "A New Dawn for Woman" and while not referring to her own personality, was really an illustration of an acquired power. The widowed mother with eight other children shed tears of joy as her daughter held the large audience of gratified white and Colored people with rapt attention. Oh yes, she will teach; she must do so for she must now help on the others. Did she pass the examination for State license to teach? Most assuredly and well, for she had been carefully trained by the AMA teachers of the Academy. She will help now to educate the others, and they need it.

This man James Sistrunk, who entered Fessenden almost full grown a dozen years ago as "Jim Sis" this year won the gold prize offered by a German for the most eloquent speech on his day of graduation. When he entered school he took hold with the little classes far far behind all who had been at school, and after a dozen years, is much of a scholar according to our standards, is a good carpenter and manager of a tailor shop which he himself owns. He has had all kinds of obstacles to overcome. His doctor told him to give up trying to finish the "course" or it would finish him. Another physician told the Principal that Sistrunk was too frail to be in school, and even the Principal advised Sistrunk to stop for a year, but Sistrunk said, "No, I shall not stop."

…It was he who became President of the YMCA, President of the Beard Literacy Society, best student in class; first-rate carpenter, director of boys, a leader and a MAN. What a lesson he has taught us of determination, patient perseverance and successful purpose and noble character.[93]

And then suddenly, Joseph Wiley disappeared without a trace. On July 1, 1915, Wiley drove to Ocala to see a movie and never returned. His car was found unharmed, his bank accounts were in order, and there was no justifiable reason for his departure.[94] Months later, in September of that year, *The Ocala Evening News* would report that Wiley had good investments and was comparatively well off. Josephine Wiley, distressed and grieving, returned to Tennessee. Rumors of tensions between Wiley and AMA Secretary Douglass came to light amid this tragic loss. Some say Wiley capitulated to Douglass, resigned, and ran off. Others speculated that Wiley may have abandoned his family and the school to live a life as a white person. Wiley's friends and those who knew him best feared the worst. According to the National Memorial on Peace and Justice, between the founding of the Union School in 1868 and 1912, there were thirteen separate incidents of lynching in Marion County. These are the known incidents of extra-judicial violence. February and December of 1915, the year of Wiley's disappearance, saw another two Black men slaughtered in Marion County. Eventually, another AMA teacher would assume Wiley's position as Principal of Fessenden Academy. With no closure and no guarantee of safety, the school persevered nonetheless.

(left) A 1914 photo of Fessenden Academy faculty. Joseph Wiley is seated second from the left in the back row. (right) I portrait of Joseph Wiley, date unknown. Source: Fessenden Academy archives maintained by Amistad Research Center, New Orleans, LA.

(left) Ferdinand Stone Fessenden. Fessenden Academy and Industrial School Catalog, 1900-1901. 1900. State Archives of Florida, Florida Memory. <https://www.floridamemory.com/items/show/333858>, accessed 1 November 2025.v(right) Frederick James Fessenden. The Fessenden School archives.

CHAPTER 3

In May 2023, former Massachusetts Senator, Democratic Party candidate for U.S. President, and U.S. Secretary of State John F. Kerry and I were on the same flight from Boston to Washington, DC. Kerry arrived at the gate with one escort and very little fanfare a few minutes before boarding. As he spoke with the airline staff members, I sensed that they shared a familiarity one might expect of a frequent flyer using the same terminal and seeing the same crew. Most ordinary passengers, like myself, were aware of his status and presence that day but remained respectful of his space and time. For a moment, I considered introducing myself. I imagined asking if I could show him something and presenting what has become my favorite image from the Fessenden Academy archives. The 1914 black-and-white photo rivals the elegance of any treasured portrait of its time. But it is more than that. The juxtaposition of a name, legacy, and race begs for an explanation, certainly not in Florida. But, just as an enlarged, gold-framed reprint startles visitors new to my office in Massachusetts, I presume that Secretary Kerry would have had questions.

For starters, who am I, and what do I do at Fessenden? Well, I am a teacher and an administrator. But what does a director of equity and inclusion do at an all-boys school in the suburbs of Boston? There are technical answers informed by the needs of the community, the national standards established by accrediting organizations, and the best practices sourced from peer schools, but the response can be simplified. Equity practitioners, when present, do what they are allowed to do. I spend time with colleagues and students learning about our differences, repairing harm when it occurs, and I help to advance the institution in ways that are not always apparent. Mostly, I ask questions because asking the right question is more important than giving the right answer, especially for those questions that challenge ideas about one's self. In a nutshell, this is the legacy I hope to leave at The Fessenden School. Long before I arrived, Secretary Kerry attended this same school in 1956 as a boarding student during an era when all of his schoolmates and teachers were white. Diversity, equity, and inclusion hadn't become a priority, but honesty and hard work were school values from the beginning. The first seventy years of school history are notably different from the last fifty, and it is with honesty, compassion, and respect that I offer a different voice.

The school that young John Kerry encountered was one of family, firmness, and pride. He stayed for one year, and when he was promoted to high school a year later, a local third-grade boy was admitted who would break the Black color barrier. For Senator Kerry, much like many others affiliated with The Fessenden School, I suspect that the image of thirteen Black girls posing in beautiful gowns just above the words Fessenden Academy would trigger some cognitive dissonance. At the airport, I passed on the opportunity to introduce myself and strike up a conversation about Fessenden memories with Senator Kerry, partly because I was nervous, partly because boarding school memories are not all alike. We all carry scars, and I have learned to take special care when navigating the past. I have also learned to appreciate that we are the *invisible men* as 1953 National Book Award winner Ralph Ellison described.

Institutional legacies are a project of remembering what is sustainable. Named buildings, framed portraits, endowed awards, and continuing established traditions are intentional acts to serve the institution by reflecting the greatness of the past. Naturally, these are selective memories passed down as a legacy to inspire. However, for the individual, our minds are wired to recall the extremes of our experiences, the very good and the very bad. I see students move beyond their mistreatment every day, and I know some adults have healed from the abuse and neglect of their childhood. And, tragically, I know others who can never be whole again. Acknowledging this contrast, the prevailing love for The Fessenden School centers on bonds of brotherhood, memories of a community of families living and working together, and gratitude to teachers. Secretary Kerry fits somewhere within this mosaic, but even with all his accomplishments and the many accolades of The Fessenden School, this story is about those Black Fessenden students he never met. Those men whose invisibility is less about a violent American society and more about memory. To understand the color barrier at Fessenden, we need to discuss how the school was founded.

Fredrick James Fessenden, born in 1862, is a seventh-generation descendant of the Fessenden patriarch Nicholas Fessenden, who arrived in America during the 1660s. As a child, Frederick moved from Lunenburg, Massachusetts, to Lockport, New York, where he attended high school. Frederick enjoyed a close relationship with his mother, whose firm guidance accompanied her immense pride in his school's success. Finances posed a problem for the family, so during the 1880s, Frederick found work in a bank to help offset the cost of attending Williams

College. He graduated with a desire to work with young students and showed tremendous potential as a Latin and Greek teacher. In 1889, Frederick began a nine-year tenure at the Berkeley School in New York, where he started a family with his bride, Emma Hart.

Emma Hart is the oldest daughter of Elizur Kirke Hart, a well-known banker and former US congressman from Albion, New York. Occasionally, Frederick would visit his parents in nearby Lockport, and a chance meeting at a social gathering paved the way for the promising union between Emma and Frederick. While at Berkeley, the family grew with the arrival of Hart and Louise Fessenden. Raising a family against the backdrop of a preparatory school was not only Fredrick and Emma's choice, but it was also consistent with the norms of the time. In particular, male instructors were encouraged to model traditional family values alongside their duties in the classroom. Wives were expected to tend to the home, the children, and the needs of their husbands and, as customary, aid in the day-to-day operation of the school. Emma and the children shared in the school experience at every step in Frederick's journey, including in 1898 when the family moved to Pottstown, Pennsylvania, where Fredrick took a position at the Hill School.

From his early days as a teacher, Frederick upheld the popular standard of discipline. The harsh nature of preparatory schools at the turn of the eighteenth century would draw public ire today. Schools embraced a brand of scholastic rigor and punishment, which often went hand in hand. Marked by strictly enforced dress codes and demerit systems, the goal was student compliance with and adherence to a particular ethic. The Hill School years were pivotal for Frederick. His experience with older boys convinced him of the importance of elementary education, and with the proper support, he was eager to start a school of his own.[95]

Dr. Harlan Amen, the principal of Phillips Exeter Academy, was an early supporter of Frederick's vision. Recognizing the need for improved training for ninth-grade boys entering Exeter, Dr. Amen contributed his time and resources. Frederick's vision for a new school would have the blessing of one of the nation's leading secondary school educators, allowing his focus to remain on fundraising and finding a location. Frederick, his father, James Walker Fessenden, and Dr. Amen first considered an option in Exeter, New Hampshire. However, desiring a more central location, they continued their search near Boston. Adding to the risk of this endeavor, the practice of sending younger boys to a boarding school was rare for American families and still unproven. With his family's savings and a loan from Dr. Amen, Frederick took a leap of faith. He purchased nine acres of land, accompanied by a white southern colonial house atop a hill with a long driveway in West Newton, Massachusetts, as the site for his school.

Yearly tuition for boarding students was set between $600 and $800, equivalent to just over $22,000 today. Investing in the education of an heir was sound logic, but The Fessenden School offered an opportunity to prepare a son to inherit both position and power. The patronage of wealthy and politically connected families was essential to the school's growth from its humble beginnings. Another undeniable factor in understanding the infancy of this soon-to-be institution is the absence of opposition. Individual sacrifice notwithstanding, Frederick seized upon the opportunity afforded to him by race, religion, and class, which, in many regards, became the value proposition to families seeking a school for their son. "It will be the aim of this school to train a boy along right lines from the beginning," wrote Dr. Amen in the school's first catalog. "To teach him how to study and form correct habits of work, and to inculcate the principles which are to regulate his daily conduct and guide his future life."

A family affair from the outset, the Fessendens took control of the West Newton property in July 1903. They planned to open the school by September, which required converting a mansion and a former golf course into a boarding school with classrooms and dormitories. Frederick's parents, Lane and James Walker, agreed to assist with housekeeping and ground maintenance. Mrs. Emma Hart Fessenden, a Vassar College graduate, had the honor and distinction of teaching the boys English literature, spelling, and grammar. On September 23, 1903, Emma wrote to her mother in New York: "The school opens with eleven boys— eight boarders and three day pupils. The carriages have been rolling up and down the hill all day."

The first class of students and their families all had some connection to Frederick or Emma, but even without these ties, future families showed the utmost confidence in the Fessenden family's ability to care for their sons. Well before the advent of websites and video conferencing, first impressions were the only impressions. Upon arrival at school, students found themselves in a completely unfamiliar environment filled with new peers, expectations, and with Frederick and Emma as the primary caregivers. *In loco parentis*, a Latin phrase translating to *in place of a parent*, remains both a legal doctrine and a foundational boarding school tenet. The Fessenden family welcomed the charge of caring for each boy as if he were their own. In these early days of the school's history, with little to no staff or faculty, responsibilities for all the students' needs fell to Emma, Frederick, and their parents. Everything, from classroom teaching to meals and laundry, required the family's attention and care. The Fessenden children, Hart and Louise, became just as much a part of the experience as any other enrolled student. The program included athletic competitions, mandatory prayer services, trips to local areas of interest, study time, nighttime stories, and talent shows, all of which took place with everyone living under one roof.

From that first group of eleven boys, one could say the school was racially diverse. George Ii Brown, born in Honolulu, was a boy of mixed ancestry. His father, Charles A. Brown, descended from John Lyons, who settled in Roxbury in 1642. His mother, Irene Kahalelaukoa ʻĪʻī Brown Holloway, was the highly respected daughter of Judge John ʻĪʻī, a prominent figure and advisor in the Hawaiian monarchy. As is typical today, the Browns discovered The Fessenden School by word of mouth, and likely chose to anglicize the spelling and pronunciation of their name. More accurately, it was family proximity that brought the Browns to Fessenden. The parents of Henry K. Hyde, Frederick's college roommate, a close confidant, and the school's first principal investor, were well-known Congregationalist missionaries in Oahu, Hawaii. Said to help convert more than 50,000 members to the church, the Hydes were deeply committed to the success of English schools on the islands, namely by serving in leadership roles at the Punahou School and several other conservatories.[96] In that capacity, the Hydes advised Irene to consider The Fessenden School as good preparation for George's matriculation at Phillips Exeter Academy. A few years later, George's brother, Francis Hyde Ii Brown, also came to Fessenden before attending the Hill School.[97]

The Browns embody some of the complexities of race and class within the school context. The boys proudly identified as Hawaiian, but much like the first Fessenden school in Florida, the role of Christian missionary work is very apparent. In this case, Charles Hyde, Henry's father, was a student of theology who quickly received his call to the ministry. From the farmlands of New York to valedictorian at Williams College to the pulpits of Massachusetts, Charles Hyde committed his life to religious and intellectual pursuits. Even when the country broke into a war between slaveholding factions and those preserving the Union, Charles continued his ministry while assisting Northern troops when he could. Following the war, the same religious fervor that led churchgoers to fundraise for Black schools in the South compelled Charles to accept a mission to Christianize the native people of Hawaii. In this way, religion and schooling, again, become dual projects of patriarchal transformation.

The Browns' grandfather, John 'Ī'ī, born in 1800, is an important figure in Hawaiian cultural memory. His writings tell the story of a young boy bound by tradition to serve the royal family through the succession of kings to the United States' annexation of the island nation. He proved himself trustworthy and astute, which curried favor, status, and family pride. Before embracing Christianity as a teenager, 'Ī'ī observed the island's indigenous rituals and costumes. When the young monarch ascended the throne, the process of Christian conversion accelerated, and under the threat of death, 'Ī'ī wrestled with the abolition of the old faith. By 1819, 'Ī'ī was among the first

Hawaiians to experience American missionary schooling and earnestly adopted their teachings. His only child, Irene, would inherit his land and wealth and continue on his path of education and service to the children of Hawaii. Upon 'Ī'ī's passing, Irene lived in the home of Charles Hyde and attended the schools the Hydes helped establish.[98]

Francis, who carries the Hyde name as a testament to his mother's close connection, and his older brother George were born and raised in Hawaii. As young men, they appear to be like any other students in the annals of The Fessenden School's early history. Phenotypically indistinguishable from peers and well-adjusted to the norms, their racial difference, while acknowledged, appears slightly mitigated by their social rank. Indeed, a child's last name and family's position often determine how they are treated. Class will give cover for race until it does not, and one's ability to pass as white is a privilege. Greatly advanced by Harvard intellectuals just a few miles away in Cambridge, efforts to maintain the purity of the white race were quickly developing into a pseudoscience by the time the Browns arrived at Fessenden. Ideas went so far as to legislate a person out of whiteness by their bloodline, last name, hair texture, eye color, and skin tone, to name a few. In this environment, it is unclear if the Brown boys experienced any form of intolerance at Fessenden. From a record-keeping perspective, it is noteworthy that for the next fifty years, the school was effectively colorblind, except for a few exceptions.

The Fessenden School, then and now, takes pride in educating boys from different lands. Today, the presence of students of color in historically white private schools, such as Fessenden, still prompts a question: how did you come to hear about this school? Mostly, folks have learned not to ask this aloud. However, I have come to appreciate that the thought, depending on the tone, while distasteful, is also historically valid and unavoidable, if not from school officials, active students, and their families, then certainly from my own community. How did you come to hear about that school? A seemingly benign remark reveals the original flaw, the defaulting identity, the unspoken truth of race and class. For the Browns, the question was answered by a few degrees of separation from the school's founder. For Black boys, it would take several decades and a shifting global and national landscape before the question would be entertained.

In the subsequent years, The Fessenden School experienced a tremendous expansion of its program and legacy. Enrollment dictated a rapid growth in the number of faculty and staff. Men and women who came to share in Frederick and Emma's dream brought New England school values and their subject matter knowledge. By residing on campus, raising families of their own, and teaching students, cultural hegemony flowed in one direction. As the physical plant transformed into a campus, the school's reputation grew with the success of each graduating class. Frederick closely followed the journeys of his students from secondary school to university, through to their professional careers. He reinforced this pride by regularly reading letters of accomplishment to the boys. "His loyalty to the alumni was boundless," Katharine Fessenden, Frederick's daughter-in-law, would later recount in her history of the school. "A dyed-in-the-wool Democrat, he never failed to vote the straight Democratic ticket unless an alumnus was on the ballot. Then, no matter what party or office, he voted for him."[99]

The 1910s were a period of stability for the school, despite multiple Fessenden boys serving in World War I. At least eighty alumni, including Frederick's son, Hart, are remembered for their sacrifice to the country. The day-to-day program continued to evolve with a faculty of roughly twenty adults. The student body grew from eleven to more than 150 by the 1920s. Paddling was introduced as a disciplinary consequence, perhaps to replicate the regimented control of those early classes. Understood to be a sound practice in rearing boys, the Fessenden family encouraged this practice much like they encouraged study hall, field trips, mentoring, poetry, athletics, and stage plays. While inculcating independence and individual thought, students received constant messages to abide by the rules and perform tasks as directed. Teachers, in fact, were called masters, and students were under their charge. Students, of course, bemoaned this structure, especially the disciplinary consequences, while parents and graduates, who often sent their sons and grandsons, recall a firm but fair upbringing that proved effective in life.

Passing tradition along to one's son was the theme, and for the Fessendens, destiny had it for Hart to take over the school from his father. After the war, Hart married Katharine Tighe, and the couple moved into a newly constructed building on campus. With the tragic passing of James Walker Fessenden, Hart relinquished some of his teaching responsibilities to Katharine so he could help his father manage the school. In January 1930, Frederick appointed a Board of Trustees to advise the newly endowed institution. Serving as the Assistant Headmaster, Hart joined his parents on the Board, which consisted of Winthrop M. Crane Jr., whose family's business holds a manufacturing patent on the US dollar; Chester Hanford, Dean of Harvard College;

Sinclair Weeks, mayor of Newton, MA; and, serving as president, was family friend Henry Hyde. What started as a family affair was now a leading institution known for educational excellence and made in the image of the founding family.

By far, the most trying time for the school came in 1935, when news of Mrs. Emma Fessenden's sudden death reached her family and the greater school community. Aging and coping with his loss, Frederick completed the school year but officially announced that Hart would be the school's headmaster moving forward. Mother to many, Emma was irreplaceable in the hearts of everyone at school, especially her birth children and husband. For thirty years, her gracefulness had presided over what was both her home and her dining room, as well as her entertaining areas and the functional space for special events and daily comings and goings. As the first lady of the school, she had a hand in every detail, from the decor of the hallways to the decorum of the students passing through them. The season of her passing provided an opportunity for school leaders to consider a proper memorial. They landed on a fitting honor for the school's first English teacher: parents and alumni generously gave to erect the Emma Hart Fessenden Library in her name.

Day-to-day operations now fell to Hart's leadership, along with the maintenance of a national profile of Frederick's making. Away from campus, Hart absorbed his father's position as a founding member of the Secondary Education Examination Board (SEB). Upon Frederick's retirement from the SEB, the chairman, Arthur Roberts of St. George's School, wrote to Frederick: "You must feel joy when you know that the organization which you largely created is so firmly founded that it can continue vigorously as a monument of your far-seeking wisdom and constant care." From 1923 to 1939, Frederick pushed the board to establish standardized examinations as a requirement for admission to secondary schools. Frederick also aligned his efforts with Harvard's Psycho-Educational Clinic, which allowed Fessenden to become one of the first schools to utilize IQ testing. Both Fessenden men were appointed treasurers and executive committee members, with Hart serving until the 1962 merger that led to the formation of the NAIS (National Association of Independent Schools). Hart and several Fessenden faculty played important roles on subject committees throughout their tenure. All in all, nearing the midpoint of the twentieth century, Hart positioned himself and the school for decades of success.

By its fiftieth year, The Fessenden School received local praise as a leading international school. In the newspaper columns and articles that circulated among peer institutions, it is evident that Fessenden was considered progressive in this area. One author went so far as to cast the school as a replica of the United Nations. Boys from Austria, Canada, China, Colombia, Cuba, Dominican Republic, Iraq, Mexico, the Netherlands, Russia, and Venezuela all called Fessenden home between 1920 and 1950. Their families were affluent, and many of the students were legacy—relatives of alumni or families who were generationally familiar with the school. Twenty-one different states were also represented among the student body. As one person close to the school put it: "Such diversity of backgrounds in its members widened horizons and made for an open-minded community. A black boy was matter-of-factly accepted as any other new boy, a deaf boy and a blind boy were welcomed and admired, friendliness and lack of prejudice the order of the day."

For others, the Fessenden School is the place where they encountered their first moment of prejudice. Black students would eventually enroll, but our definition of inclusion today would not so easily apply. Most teachers will agree that students can be unkind to one another. And I have yet to encounter an all-boys school that is free from name-calling or bullying. Any difference, be it racial, socioeconomic, religious, country of origin, language fluency, or physical ability, tends to be an easy target for jokes or worse. A closer look at Fessenden's international student population reveals the surnames of wealthy oligarchs and dictators. Did family name, reputation, and nationality offer cover or cause conflict? That is a story for a different writer. From the Fessenden family's perspective, and that of most community members, it is clear that they considered the school welcoming. Being open to boys from around the world is a powerful message. But, given the nature of private schools, that generosity came with a price.

As a point of fact, Negro schools across the United States have always demonstrated an excellent capability to educate Negro children. One cannot name a successful Black person who did not have Black teachers. Therefore, the calculus of sending a Black child to The Fessenden School would have been the same for any family, regardless of color, return on investment. The idea of paying hard-earned money for a racially hostile experience would have been considered a short-sighted dream for the few who could afford it. If local Black families were not dissuaded by fears of harm or the feeling of racial intolerance, they were certainly deterred by the cost of tuition. This is why the Black color barrier then, or socioeconomic diversity among Black families today, is the litmus test for so many private schools.

Closer to campus, Frederick was the wise leader who boosted morale and offered sage advice. When his health permitted, Frederick would spend his day walking the grounds, tutoring students, and listening to their debates. Boys engaged with such topics as: The Nations of the World Should Adopt a Plan of Complete Disarmament; Should Capital Punishment Be Abolished; and Is The Condition of the Negroes Worse Today than It Was Before the Civil War? We are left to ponder the irony. Part of developing the minds of future policymakers requires young people to explore the free market of ideas. Frederick wanted a school capable of preparing great, worldly men. For his students, most of whom were privileged and buffered from the direct consequences of the topics debated at school, their worldview began to crystallize at Fessenden.

As Frederick's health faded, he retreated to a house on campus under the care of his nurse. The sorrow expressed by his children, colleagues, and students was a testament to their love for him. Frederick was never far from his school, and he spent his final days as he had lived. In February 1943, the school said goodbye to its founder, and the tributes poured in. "The boys and men who received their early instruction from him, and the schools and colleges which are the beneficiaries of his devoted service to youth, owe more than can be expressed[100]."

Hart navigated the school through the tail end of the Great Depression and the coming of the Second World War. During these tumultuous times for the nation and the world, Fessenden continued to serve boys and their families with a steady hand. By many metrics, the school remained joyful and relatively unfazed, while the collapse of America's economy left millions destitute. Local estimates place white unemployment rates at twenty-five percent. At the same time, the national average for Black unemployment surpassed a catastrophic fifty percent. In this climate of despair, it would take the rise of fascism and military displacement to activate the school's first fundraising effort for financial aid.

Breaking the wealth barrier was neither a fluke event nor intentional. By the 1940s, no amount of public pressure could have motivated private schools to significantly change their student body or approach to student admissions. What could one say? It was, in fact, a private school. Public critique, if any, would have been rebuffed on the basis of preserving individual discretion and general acceptance of the prosperity gospel. To be wealthy was to be blessed by God and tangentially considered moral. Ultimately, The Fessenden School was a business: the service was education, the clientele included families of great stature, and the price was tuition. In these times, the school had not yet amassed an endowment to sustain ambitious outreach to marginalized communities, even if there was a desire to do so. Additionally, the value proposition to families was never one of upward mobility; most had already arrived. For these families, much of what sold the school for generations was its exclusive feel.

As career educators, the Fessenden faculty were not wealthy bankers, attorneys, politicians, or international leaders like many of their students' parents. Tuition did more than cover the cost of education; it operated as a socioeconomic threshold. But class tensions exist even in the service of a high-end commodity such as private school education. There are consumers and producers, with gradations among them. At the most endowed schools, you will find intentionally modest facilities paired with state-of-the-art renovations, campus work programs, community service requirements, and an expectation that students refer to faculty by their honorifics. Much of this is designed to produce the humility and good character associated with a proper education. For wealthier families, it was perhaps necessary and desired. However, as private schools began to admit students needing financial aid, class hierarchy shifted. Schools have the potential to be egalitarian, but if race and racism are the most pronounced shortcomings, class and classism are the unspoken reality hiding in plain sight. Remarkably, the upheaval of the Great Depression and its regional impact on working-class families did not spark sympathies for change. It would again take proximity.

When family and friends asked Hart to assist refugees fleeing Europe, he turned to the alumni and parents of current students for their support. The response was overwhelming, and Hart was able to enroll nearly twenty scholarship boys. An untold number of students likely required some sort of financial assistance throughout the decades, but for The Fessenden School, the balance between access and affordability begins here. The families of the refugee boys, as many called them, were well connected in Belgium, England, Ireland, and Scotland. The war threatened safety and stability throughout Europe, and families of particular means found empathy among a number of New England private schools. Other students came to the States with far less. So, while schools opened their doors to students who showed promise or were especially destitute, their affinity was whiteness. At Fessenden, the boys stood out for their heavy accents and partiality to soccer and cricket over football. Otherwise, beyond their understandable homesickness, they fit nicely in the Fessenden fold and quickly became beloved community members.

The attack on the US air base at Pearl Harbor, Hawaii, on December 7, 1941, moved public sentiment from spectator sympathies to wartime allegiance. Millions of Americans tuned their radios to hear President Franklin Delano Roosevelt's Day of Infamy speech the following evening. However, First Lady Eleanor Roosevelt was the first public official to address the nation. Mrs. Roosevelt had always been outspoken; she held press conferences, maintained a weekly radio show, and shared newsworthy updates in her "My Day" column. On this occasion, she chose to empathize with her audience: "I should like to say just a word to the women in the country tonight. I have a boy at sea on a destroyer, for all I know he may be on his way to the Pacific. Two of my children are in coast cities on the Pacific. Many of you all over the country have boys in the services who will now be called upon to go into action. You have friends and families in what has suddenly become a danger zone. You cannot escape anxiety. You cannot escape a clutch of fear at your heart, and yet I hope that the certainty of what we have to meet will make you rise above these fears."[101]

Before the Allied Forces and the United States could claim victory, nearly sixteen million US citizens would serve the country in some capacity. The first lady's son, FDR Jr., and 790 Fessenden alumni were among them. Along with the 37 Fessenden men who lost their lives during the war, they would come to be known as the *Greatest Generation*. The world had changed so much; fascism was said to be defeated, and democracy and freedom were on the rise—that is, if your racial designation and class station afforded such humanity to you.

Otherwise, as in the case of more than one million Black veterans, you returned home to conditions almost as devastating as the battlefields you survived.

The Fessenden School took great pride in the service records of its sons. Since 1919, visitors to Memorial Hall, which housed the treasured schoolroom, several classrooms, and dormitories, have paid tribute to those who fought in the First World War. Throughout the 1940s, when graduates exchanged letters with Hart detailing their experiences at war, he would publicly share their remarks with students and faculty during prayer time. The class of 1946 continued the tradition of recognition and gifted an engraved memorial board carrying the names of alumni lost during the Second World War. The class of 1948 followed suit and gifted a large shield to go over the door leading to Memorial Hall. "It was known as the memorial terrace, and the boys gathered there often to chat, read, strum guitars, and softly sing," Katharine Fessenden wrote.[102]

When any group of people demonstrates their collective gratitude, a custom will likely ensue. It's one of the many ways we teach pride between generations. The Fessenden students who curated Memorial Hall with acts of service and remembrance were unaware that they were following in a long-standing Black tradition. In the United States, public war memorials originate with the freedmen. David W. Blight's book *Race and Reunion* spotlights how ten thousand Black children, women, and men in South Carolina participated in the first memorial day of its kind. In May 1865, returning home from war victorious or, in the case of the Confederates, in defeat, paled in comparison to the jubilation of being legally free. Before the dust could truly settle, it was common Black folk, moved by what they experienced, who were the first to honor the fallen.

It is worth remembering, as Blight describes, "Black Charlestonians gave birth to an American tradition. In doing so, they declared the meaning of the war in the most public way possible—by their labor, their words, their songs, their solemn parade of roses, lilacs, and marching feet." Days ahead of the memorial service, 28 Black men from the local church reorganized a mass grave of Union war prisoners who died in captivity, mostly by disease, lining the dead into orderly rows. Some 300 Black women carrying flower baskets and crosses followed the procession of 3000 newly enrolled schoolchildren. They sang "John Brown's Body" and prayed. Ministers from all the Black churches in Charleston spoke to a mixed crowd of Black and white citizens and delivered the official dedication. Afterward, Union officers, Black ministers, and abolitionist missionaries took to the grandstand to offer remarks. "A full brigade of Union infantry, including the Massachusetts 54th, 35th, and 104th U.S. Colored Troops, marched in double columns around the martyrs' graves and held a drill in the infield."[103]

The stories of Black soldiers, their families, and how they are positioned within America's cultural narrative tell us everything. From Crispus Attucks, the first martyr, to Prince and Primus Hall, the men of the Massachusetts 54th, and WWII veterans, Black Bostonians, in particular, have fought for security from all forms of oppression and the unrealized ideals of this country. The Greatest Generation would not be such without the contributions of the famed Tuskegee Airmen. The lessons we learn from this all-Black battalion of jet fighters could easily have been lost if the survivors had not insisted otherwise. One of the last surviving Tuskegee airmen, Brigadier General Enoch Woodhouse II, is a Boston native who continues to receive honors, including a newly dedicated mural located in Boston Logan Airport. In sharing part of his journey with a reporter, he recalled: "December 7, 1941, we were on our way to church. My mother said, 'Boys, America is at war. And, I want you to serve.'" Woodhouse continued, "Can you imagine a Black woman saying that? All she had in the world were her two boys. And the pictures we grew up with [were] our people being lynched."[104]

With his high school diploma in hand, Woodhouse fulfilled his mother's wish and traveled to the Deep South for the first time. The degradation of second-class citizenship existed everywhere, from the railcars to the military barracks. As Woodhouse said, "All Blacks, every Black, no matter what your education, no matter what, you were assigned to certain bases. And, you were assigned to certain squadrons." The racism from white counterparts and officers felt much like the days of the Massachusetts 54th when Black soldiers were given fewer resources, assigned menial tasks, and held back by extremely low and demeaning biases or an extremely high glass ceiling. But to each other, "we had nothing to compare ourselves with." Woodhouse says it best: "People asked me, 'How does it feel in an all-Black unit with just nothing but Black people like yourself?' I said, 'I felt fine.' Because I was with the finest men I've known in life, no matter what their race…. The real top gun in the Air Force was a Black guy."

Roughly 16,000 people served with the Tuskegee Airmen, but only a handful live with us today. To a mainstream white audience, their contributions were discounted and ignored in the years after the war. It is a hard thing to discuss openly, especially for those Black soldiers who lived through it. As a glimpse of this, Woodhouse shared: "Once in a while, we filled in guarding prisoners at Camp Utah. German prisoners of war, and incidentally, the German prisoners of war ate better than we did because of the international protocols." Years before General Woodhouse would enlist and make his way to Tuskegee, racism almost thwarted the project entirely. In 1939, President Roosevelt signed the Civilian Pilot Training Act into law. Anticipating U.S. involvement in the war, the law sought to open opportunities for technical and academic training at select universities for a new generation of pilots. Legal segregation all but ensured Black Americans and Black colleges would be barred from participating. However, the Black press and activist organizations pressured and eventually succeeded in getting the program greenlit at six HBCUs. This led to Tuskegee University being selected as the central site for Black pilot training in the nation. Racist ideas about Black people and their service in the military, or the government's role in providing Black Americans with job opportunities, especially while the white working class was just gaining traction with New Deal policies, saturated the landscape when Eleanor Roosevelt visited Tuskegee University in the spring of 1941. "The days at Tuskegee have given me much to think about," she wrote. "To see a group of people working together for improvement of undesirable conditions is very heartening." Her visit was not specifically focused on the pilot program, but rather on the hospital, where she met with Black patients and physicians. However, when the First Lady arrived, even folks in the White House considered Black people incapable of teaching aviation. Despite such animus, or perhaps because of it, Eleanor insisted on watching the Black pilots train and even disobeyed her security team by taking a flight with lead instructor Charles "Chief" Anderson. The expansive media coverage included a photo of the First Lady seated in the cockpit. Certainly, for President Roosevelt, Eleanor's experience helped move the needle. "They have advanced training here, and some of the students went up and did acrobatic flying for us. These boys are good pilots. I had the fun of going up in one of the tiny training planes with the head instructor and seeing this interesting countryside from the air."[105] The attack on Pearl Harbor occurred that winter, and the Tuskegee program, which began modestly, went on to break the color barrier, set records, and solidify a legacy by the end of World War II.

The First Lady of the United States was willing to see and treat her fellow Black citizens as equal human beings long before the overwhelming majority of the nation. For this, she became intensely polarizing. In the 1930s, Eleanor was active with the National Association for the Advancement of Colored People (NAACP) antilynching legislative efforts. She often opposed many government officials' public policy dealings with race. Important matters such as the fight against segregation in the armed forces, housing, business, and education had her public support in the face of intolerant rhetoric and political roadblocks. Eleanor spoke out against racial violence in places such as Detroit and Birmingham. She received death threats for decades and especially angered Southern Klan members, who raised a $25,000 bounty as late as the 1950s. Black commentators have remarked that Eleanor was a friend in the White House. Certainly, having educator and civil rights activist, Mary McLeod Bethune as a close personal friend and advisor is significant. I am not one to offer blanket praise for being decent. However, Eleanor's stance in the face of all this and more is noteworthy. She was not without shortcomings and bias, but for her station and time, she was nothing short of bold. Mrs. Roosevelt's visit to The Fessenden School in 1950 was less political in nature, but for the faculty and staff, it was the most memorable event. Her grandson, a boarding student, Franklin D. Roosevelt III, played proud host and took his grandmother on a tour of the campus. She spent time with Hart and the Fessenden family. Faculty enjoyed speaking with the former First Lady about Franklin's growth as well as the politics of the world. Like most things, Eleanor documented her trip to Fessenden in her publicly circulated column. A half-century of educating sons of the world's most prosperous families came with considerable notoriety. The Roosevelts were an institution in themselves, public-facing, wealthy, and service-oriented, gracefully and politically moderate for their time—perhaps America's most renowned family.

Eleanor's visit provides a measuring stick. What did mid-twentieth-century social and racial progress mean at a private school, and how did it differ from what we can observe in public schools? For all the debate over how the public and government agencies responded to race, there is much silence on how private schools reacted. What ultimately becomes the impetus for white parents to accept a Black classmate for their child, or a Black teacher? It is unclear if Eleanor expressed a desire to see Fessenden become a more diverse school for her grandson. Segregation was evil and warranted her resistance in ways that racial and class barriers did not. So, is there a difference between an all-white public school and an all-white private school? Indeed, it is easier to observe the flaw in the former, while it is easier to correct the flaw in the latter.

The Fessenden Running Boy has had an enduring presence since its design in 1925. The whimsical image symbolizes everything, including the joy of school. Two wrought-iron Running Boy signs marked the driveway entrances to school for over fifty years. Source: Along Right Lines, The Fessenden School, 1903-2003

CHAPTER 4

In November of 2020, VOICE boys at Fessenden celebrated Black Lives Matter Day with the support of classmates and their faculty.

I do not look like the running type, and before 2020, I would be the first to question how anyone could enjoy it. As a sport, running is challenging and intimidating for newcomers, especially for someone like me who has spent much of my life avoiding the need to run. Growing up, we ran as a punishment, or because Brother So-and-So said it built character and discipline. I have vivid memories of Black men running toward something or away from someone, but never to run for the sake of running. I knew Black folks who ran competitively as part of a track team, or athletes who had to train for another sport. But hardly anyone ran for the joy of it, and few were ever spotted casually running along the side of a road or through our neighborhoods.

Call it divine or a minor miracle, but it was not foreseeable that a once 320-pound non-athlete would become a roadrunner in his late thirties. I am most grateful to have the physical ability to run, the time to do so, and the support of my loved ones. In particular, I am thankful for Black Men Run (BMR) Boston, the regional chapter of a national organization founded to promote a healthy lifestyle among African American men, for their brotherhood, and for helping me explore the world of running and marathoning. Running has been a life-enhancing practice of self-care and community engagement. It has given me tremendous mental clarity through moments of failure, regret, and self-discovery. I do some of my best thinking, even my best writing, while out on a run.

Running has taught me the value of being first. Now, I will likely never take first place in a foot race. But running has taught me there is always a race, there is competition, even with oneself, and that being first matters. How much praise and distinction we give to first place depends on the context. Standing atop a podium is one way to single out individual triumph, but reminding ourselves who and what came first is another. The older I get and the more distances I attempt, the more I appreciate the meaning behind the saying *life is a marathon, not a sprint*. However, my time with BMR has also reinforced for me that life is, in fact, a relay. The intentional ways BMR Boston brings history to light during our neighborhood runs and how we discuss issues facing our community as fathers and sons underscore this.

Seeing life as a relay came into sharper focus when I participated in the Civil Rights Race Series' Selma to Montgomery 51 Mile Relay, commemorating the renowned 1965 Voting Rights March. We crossed the infamous Edmund Pettus Bridge and ended as a team, along with hundreds of other cyclists and runners, at the steps of the Montgomery State House. The lessons are countless. I was awe-struck by the thought of following the same path as those brutalized on Bloody Sunday, March 7, 1965, my sneakers treading along a road paved by church shoes, conviction, and deep community organizing. Nearly sixty years ago, this route was lined by unapologetic racists, camera crews, and reporters from around the world as common Black folk risked their lives and livelihoods in pursuit of basic human rights and dignity. Now, there I was, with my newly found brothers, tackling our individual segments in relative peace, silently reflecting, as our voices were lost to cheering, pacing, competing, and willing ourselves on to the next checkpoint. Relays remind us that success is not individual, that we belong to something larger. Relays help us appreciate that even when we are unaware, we are not alone. Relays, much like life itself, demand we do our very best in our specific time and space. And when we press forward and cannot see behind us, relays remind us that someone passed the baton forward, and someone came first.

Institutions in the United States, including independent schools, preserve a story of who came first to suit particular outcomes. It is kind to say that the popular narratives we learn as children are selective. In reality, misplacing the truth is hardly a coincidence for the same institutions that are hell-bent on documentation and commemoration. Power understands that a people's legacy rests within the memory of who came first. I come from enslaved people who came from great societies and kingdoms before European interruption. The struggle over curriculum is a struggle over memory.

"Power concedes nothing without a demand. It never did, and it never will." When Frederick Douglass wrote these words, he could not have imagined today's battles over our national origin story, which materialize into a debate over curriculum. We have not arrived here without a moral and physical struggle, yet because we lack the transmission of memory, we lack progress in the most essential ways. The great James Baldwin reminds us, "To be African American is to be African without memory, and American without privilege." What a privilege it must be to have memory. What a tragedy it is to have memory taken away. And what a failure it must be not to learn from memory.

With opposition to teaching a fuller, more accurate national history again on the upswing, schools must learn to draw lessons from within. New England-based private schools excel at relaying a dominant white aesthetic to succeeding generations by default. Their histories, much like the history of the country, have been written by a homogenous group of individuals. It rarely crosses the mind to question what has been preserved or the traditions held so dearly. To ask whose name is on this building and who they were to each of us feels taboo. When the discourse around curriculum intensifies, revisit the history of school; the answers are all there, we only need to ask who came first and why. Placing institutional memory within the context of a larger national or even global history is the progress that is too often overlooked.

At my first independent school, the history of the founding family is not taught, and few bother to ask if, or how, members interacted with Black people in their time. Not much is mentioned about the school's first Black students. Nonetheless, the institution remains committed to recruiting and retaining Black students. It did not take me long to observe that one could be considered brilliant, or a school could tout academic excellence, and be completely ignorant of Black history. This ignorance stems from omission and is rooted in a particular priority. If chattel slavery is one of the original sins of this nation, silence from an institution founded during that era invites many questions and, indeed, a spiritual disharmony. Centuries of polish provide little ease.

What did this family name mean to Black people before me? While I didn't learn about abolition or slaveholding, I did learn about the history of Black faculty and students fighting for visibility and working to improve the school. My tenure in the Office of Multicultural Affairs follows a relay that includes Rosanna Salcedo, who succeeded Russell Witherspoon, who followed Mark Blackman, who accepted the role after Veda Robinson. Predating all of us was James Montford, a man who, I am sure, brought many talents to the Academy and supported students in ways I can only imagine. I will never forget learning how this educator underwent a six-day hunger strike as a social protest to convince his colleagues—the faculty and the school's administration—to support a plan to recognize Dr. Martin Luther King Jr.'s birthday as a school holiday. I recall learning that years later, a handful of Black faculty members organized a single-line march through the town of Exeter to acknowledge Dr. King's birthday, which the state of New Hampshire refused to observe until the year 2000. All of this occurred in the face of overt acts throughout the decades. I recall each of us, student and adult, balancing the weight of racist encounters, imposter syndrome, and survivor's guilt against this golden opportunity for upward mobility. I recall that there were no buildings named after a Black person. I remember a single painting of a Black faculty member erected in the historic auditorium. I recall that there was no official curriculum that taught about the rich legacy left by Black alumni or faculty. I recall that it took leadership changes and a student-led sit-in to muster the will to hire a Director of Equity and Inclusion. I recall the terminations, the contracts not renewed, and the promotions denied. I recall Black faculty members attempting to support one another when the institution fell short. I remember it being imperfect. I remember the exhaustion.

My institutional memory did not contain a complete list of names or the name of the first Black faculty member, but the themes were evident. And the experience of Black students and faculty was consistently taxing among independent schools across the country. Opposition will always be present. Someone broke the color barrier and paid a significant toll; all others are to pay it forward.

Heading into the winter of 2021, a Black parent asked me quite frankly if I knew the name of the first Black student to attend The Fessenden School. Black History Month was quickly approaching, and the parent thought this history would be a great thing to highlight for her son and his class. I had no clue. Perhaps more alarmingly, I never thought to inquire. At the time, given my knowledge of Fessenden, Exeter, and all other independent schools, I was confident that the story of the first Black student would be anticlimactic. Pioneering Black people learn to survive in toxic environments, and the result of that conditioning often manifests in something unhealthy for the person or unsustainable for others. There is, unfortunately, little balance. I was somewhat familiar with the history of Black teachers at the school and the parent- and faculty-led push to create the job I held. But I was not eager to hear what I assumed to be a decontextualized story of the first Black student struggling through a sea of whiteness without support. I certainly was not interested in hearing his story in mixed company or framed by others. I wanted to hear it from the source.

White schools have taught me to read the audience as much as I listen to the speaker. When we speak, the paralysis, the shock, the disbelief, the outrage, the reflexive troubleshooting, the sudden sorrow, the whataboutism, the pseudo-intellectualism, the virtue signaling, the difference, it all captures my attention. I used to judge Black folk, including myself, quite harshly for not producing the results most needed with our words. I could not appreciate, then, how we are all a product of engaging with an audience that cannot fully see or hear us. Selective sight and hearing make authentic communication physically draining. And finally, there is usually a percentage of the audience too familiar with Black trauma, Black subservience, and Black grievance. Familiar in a way that they are unmoved, literally or metaphorically, there are no new words, only new people with new stories that come as routinely as a new school year.

I learned to lower my standards and stopped asking the questions I thought I knew the answers to. I was convinced that Black people cannot be whole at a white school. I gave up trying years ago. Instead, I coped with a firm resolve to compartmentalize, to prioritize reciprocity, and to code-switch until I returned home or until I found a battle worth fighting. I also came to respect the fact that other Black people need to reach this discovery in their own way. This was growth for me, leaving scars behind. But I was now working to support boys as young as five. I could not sit back and wait for the rude awakening of anti-Blackness to reach them. On the other hand, proactively teaching these boys the skills to navigate race can look like paranoia. To them, the topic of racism is foreign until it becomes intimate, and then it feels like it's a little too late. It is a daunting thing to tell a fourth-grader not to believe the racist joke of a classmate. Even a callused mind will empathize and grieve for the loss of innocence. I wish I could share all the ways Black people resist and defend our dignity, but they do not allow those courses at white institutions until graduate school. Some Black parents are convinced by what white schools say. Others find ways to convince themselves. This parent's question about the first Black student was not a critique of the school, but rather a desire to relay memory for her child, and I needed that wake-up call.

The question specifically came to me. Given that I had only been on the job for a few months, I understood this to be evidence of the importance and newness of my role. It was also a testament to the tangible gains that affinity spaces provide. There is an undeniable awkwardness to the question, and the answer is not something I would use generally for marketing. Still, I wanted to believe that the curiosity had not escaped many others, regardless of race, over the years. My first step was to turn to colleagues with more tenure than I. Unfortunately, no Black faculty had been at Fessenden long enough to recall, so I inquired with those who had the most institutional memory.

"That's an interesting question."

"Have you spoken with so-and-so?"

"I actually don't know."

"We don't have clear records from that period."

"Do you know about George Ii?"

My journey to find the first Black Fessenden student started a full year before I realized that the first Fessenden school was a Black school in Florida, so the full gravity of the question had not yet revealed itself. At the time, I felt troubled when it appeared that the question was unresolved—that is, until I tried to answer it for myself. In Massachusetts, official records dating back to the 1950s and beyond were maintained modestly on the school grounds. However, the living institutional memory available to me through retirees and long-standing faculty members dates back to the '70s and '80s. In the decades spanning the school's archived history and the oral history I could access, there are gaps, lost narratives, and general colorblindness. Which is to say that whiteness was the default, so there was no need for a paper trail of racial data for each student. Any official reference to a student's physical and mental traits would appear during the application phase, if at all. International addresses, non-anglicized surnames, letters from graduates living abroad, and distinguishable phenotypes were the only markers of difference. Drawing a conclusion here was not an exact science, but after sifting through binders of black-and-white school photos, student records, and dozens of interviews, I understood the challenge to be both clerical and reflective of the times. I hoped to find a clear record of the first Black child to walk the halls of The Fessenden School. I knew it was noteworthy, but after weeks of searching, I had to consider whether a family might choose not to be called first. Or, if the school's position to limit a paper trail of identifiable characteristics, primarily included a student's race and ethnicity, for good reason. The task was daunting, and I struggled with my own limitations. How could something so simple be so evasive? But before my concerns could grow, a colleague offered some context and encouragement: "I'm certain that our first Black student was Craig Lovell, but he wasn't our first Black graduate."

With no caption accompanying the image, a single, suspected photo of Craig Lovell as a Fessenden student sits in the archives. Others were confident that the small, third-grade boy pictured was indeed him—he fit the description. I was not the first employee to research this question. I was the latest, and after a deep review of the same records, albeit some years apart, I reached the same conclusion. Craig was the first self-identifying Black boy in the school's history. I studied the files long enough to support that assertion, but I did not have a direct connection to the Lovell family to make a formal acknowledgment. In the winter of 2021, I pursued the angle by email, phone calls, and LinkedIn messages. It had been years since Craig last communicated with the school, and I was excited to share how Fessenden was changing in really positive ways. I wrote, "Mr. Lovell, I found your name in my work with The Fessenden School. I hope you won't mind me reaching out this way, but I'd love to connect with you soon." I left my official school email address, office line, and personal cell phone number, but received no response.

That Black parent never got an answer from me. When we crossed paths again, I spoke on behalf of the school and assured her that we were close to making a determination. In reality, I had hit a wall, and there was little motivation to press forward. What should have been a question for all felt like a Black people issue, which felt like a DEI matter, which ultimately meant it was a me-problem. Having a name and picture was progress, but by now, I was invested in hearing Craig's story, pulling lessons from it, and meeting the first Black student. Unfortunately, I had a full plate of responsibilities, and nobody was asking for this connection to happen, at least not in the way I had imagined it should occur. I also had good reason to fear that Craig's time at Fessenden might make him reluctant to engage. This was my experience at a previous private school, and few things are as universal as Black people and the complex relationships we have with white institutions and spaces. There were Black alums who relished their time at school, and there were Black alums who hated the racism they endured from some people within the student body, faculty, and especially, the town, but they would not trade being a graduate for the world. For them, there is pride in belonging and in overcoming. And there are others so deeply wounded and filled with regret that they vowed never to step foot on campus again, far less to recommend a neighbor or send their own child. These graduates are now adults, and while all parents pass along their cautions, Black parents must decide if the risk of placing a child in harm's way outweighs the reward gained from perseverance.

***

In 1957, when Mrs. Lovell, born Oral Louis MacPherson, and her husband, Dr. Ronald E. R. Lovell, decided to transfer their son from the local public elementary school to Fessenden, they did so as trailblazers in their own right. The couple's youngest son, Craig, was born Ronald Craig Remington Lovell in 1948. Applying to Fessenden required a transfer of school records, a medical examination, letters of reference from reputable sources, an aptitude test, a family interview, and significant financial resources. An internal memo reads, "They [Dr. and Mrs. Lovell] brought their son around Saturday afternoon to see the school. He is a Negro who teaches at the Tufts Dental School. The boy is currently in the third grade but won't be nine until November 30th. I pointed out that he probably belonged in the third grade next year, unless he were exceptionally able. The parents were perfectly willing to go along with this. Dr. Lovell is a very fine-looking person, and Mrs. Lovell is unusually attractive. The boy is a little youngster with the characteristic curly hair."

Mrs. Lovell was the daughter of a prominent Chicago dentist, who was a veteran of WWI and a native of British-controlled Guyana. Dr. Lovell shared a homeland and profession with his father-in-law, and both men established successful practices during their time in the States. Race-conscious U.S. immigration has always preferred whiteness over all, so it's hard to know how much agency Craig's father and grandfather had when recording their racial backgrounds on census documents. Both men received their initial training under the British system and graduated from American universities when few Negros were able. For Dr. Lovell, beginning in 1937, dentistry was a second career after setting track and field records as the single representative from Guyana during the British Empire Games.

The summer of 1940 saw Dr. Lovell complete his studies at Northwestern University, his marriage to Mrs. Lovell, and his appointment to the faculty of Howard University.[106] By the mid-1950s, the family had relocated to Massachusetts, where Dr. Lovell took a teaching position at Tufts University.

For grade school pupils, letters of reference have little to do with a student's readiness for the rigor of a private school. The purpose is to determine fit-ness. Will this prospective family fit in with our other families, and, by proxy, will the boy fit in with our program? The strength of a family's name and their connections make this multilayered assessment that much easier. A marathon of steps disadvantaging all but well-positioned families has become more complex since the 1950s. One letter from Dr. Lovell's colleague, Dr. Ralph Wheeler, stands out:

If Craig develops into exactly one-half the man that his father did he will be quite the person! Lovell senior is one of the leading dental teachers in the country: exact in his standards and loved by his students. He does an active practice of dentistry on the side and from personal experience I can testify that his work is nearly perfect as present methods can make them. He does about twice in his practice as the average practitioner and keeps two offices going through long hours. He makes his own fillings—doesn't send this work out to dental laboratories. He charges more but because he is a fast worker I have found him less expensive than other top-flight men. In spite of his many achievements (he was an Olympic high jumper for British Guiana among other things), he remains modest and unassuming – much more so than most white people with less to their credit. He is so intelligent that those who meet him forget his color in the first few moments of conversation with him as his neighbors in

Newton have already forgotten the consternation his arrival caused.

Mrs. Lovell has been, in her way, as much a community asset as her husband has in his. She is a tireless worker for community enterprises and as generous as she is efficient. She has a better and less emotional attitude toward race problems than anyone I know, white or colored. She has studied the problem from aspects I never knew existed and it has given her a balanced philosophy not only on that subject but in many others as well.

If race questions are raised in connection with Craig's admission to Fessenden the family will straighten them out. You and the school administration won't have to do so.

Dr. Wheeler signed his letter and addressed it to the school's admissions office. In a short span of time, Craig's file was complete and ready for review. This letter is significant because it provides the clearest demonstration of the various ways in which race operates. Whereas internal documentation was understandably ambiguous, a third-party perspective sheds important light. Between April and May of 1957, Hart Fessenden, the school's headmaster, communicated with the Lovells about Craig's grade-level placement and the recent receipt of his scores. There is no mention of a scholarship, special program, or accommodations that would not apply to other students. And just like that, without applause or protest, the tacit language between Hart and the Lovells confirmed Craig's admission and signaled the quiet shattering of a Black color barrier.

These findings give meaning to the phrase a needle in a haystack. I was left to wonder if the needle was buried, lost, or even a needle in the first place. There is no public record suggesting that The Fessenden School ever denied admission to a Black boy based on his race. And we will likely never know if any other Black family gave strong consideration to applying before 1957. It is clear from Dr. Wheeler's letter that colorblindness was a choice, a flawed and potentially harmful one, but a choice common for the era. Perhaps, behind closed doors, among the faculty, students, and their families, there was verbal acknowledgment, support, debate, disfavor, worry, doubt, disgust, anger, or even joy expressed. But there is no school record of it. Hart, of all people, would have the autonomy to admit families as he saw fit. Still, to attribute the unlikeliness of the Lovells and the relative silence that followed to blanket discretion felt incomplete. And it was. For months, I continued to search, inquire, and scour for artifacts or anything that could substantiate my feelings about the Lovells or demonstrate some intentionality on the school's behalf. In the thousands of pages of archived notes, there is a single mention of race by school officials dated June 20, 1956:

There was a discussion of questions relating to the admission of negro students, and it was the unanimous opinion of the meeting that negro students should neither be sought nor denied admission when fully qualified to enter into the life of the school.

There being no further business the meeting adjourned at 6:15 PM.

It was chilling to read, and my mind raced with questions. As I pondered this note, I wondered how it all unfolded. What sparked this final business of the day in the last meeting of the year? The Lovells' first visit to Fessenden occurred in March of 1957, almost a full year away, so was this all coincidental? Was there an inquiry beforehand, or was this question raised in reference to another family? Had the question of negro admission truly been unresolved for years, and was this the record of an official ruling? The purpose of the note was to preserve memory, but for whom? I went back through the archives to search for similar discussions on the potential admission of international students, as well as Jewish, Asian, Arab, or Hispanic students, faculty children, and even students in need of financial aid. This clause was indeed unique. The explicit statement not to deny admission is all the more telling when one considers the era. For Black students and their families, the environment at Fessenden was turning from avoidance to tolerance.

History grants us some perspective on what it means for Black people to break a color barrier. We can turn to the works of Anna Julie Cooper and the legacy of Martin Delaney in ways that the Fessenden decision-makers perhaps could not. By 1957, Dr. Cooper was a ninety-nine-year-old living icon of Black education. Only the fourth African American woman to earn a PhD, Dr. Cooper was born enslaved in Raleigh, North Carolina. Her illustrious career took her from being a gifted young child at St. Augustine's Normal and Collegiate Institute to Oberlin College, where she earned both bachelor's and master's degrees.[107] She eventually became the principal of the famous Paul Laurence Dunbar High School in Washington, DC, the first public high school for Black youth. In 1892, Dr. Cooper published a collection of essays entitled *A Voice from the South: By a Black Woman from the South,* in which she posits, "The late Martin Delaney, who was an unadulterated Black man, used to say…when he entered the council of kings the black race entered with him."[108] Cooper's writing suggests that Delaney, who was an abolitionist, journalist, physician, army officer—a giant of his time—and a contemporary of Harriet Tubman and Fredrick Douglass, was aware that while admission to a select room served as a morsel of representation, the goal was to resist. Certainly, he understood that we must resist being separated from our people and positioned as a token of white progress.

Picture what it would look like for a Black child to enter school with the race, not because of their race or attached to biases about their race, but with the support of their race. For example, have you seen what happens when a Black parent shadows their child for multiple days of school? In my experience, student behaviors change, preparation methods change, teacher-student interactions change, and the curriculum may also change. Then again, this is not unique to race. Parent involvement creates change in any school. When done equitably and appropriately, the change can be effective for all, including the educators. Parents have lived experiences that transcend the textbook, and they can articulate cultural memories that complement traditional learning methods. What is special about Black parents, and specific enough for this example, is how their presence deters overt racism and shields a Black child from harm. The sort of harm that can go undetected, the sort of harm that Black parents fear.

I so desperately wanted to speak with Craig Lovell about what was true for him during his time at Fessenden. I continued to reach out on social media and through the single email address the school had maintained since the early 2010s. At the time, I had no sense of his family's history or how his parents came to decide on Fessenden. My colleagues and I would periodically cycle back to strategize how to make contact, but the dots weren't connecting.

By the spring of 2022, I had been pulled into the world of the Fessenden Academy. My research took me to the Amistad Research Center on the Tulane University campus and to a Fessenden Academy reunion in Ocala, Florida. In Massachusetts, this was all very new. Introducing a community to a much older and distant cousin school raised a hornet's nest of questions. How did you find this? Did Ferdinand and Frederick know each other? What can you tell us about the Fessenden family? Do the schools resemble each other? Can our students appreciate the racial history underpinning both schools? How much can we teach them about Reconstruction? Is Fessenden Academy still open? If the schools are not affiliated, why is this so important? Does it matter which school was established first?

In total, I gave more than forty talks, from division-wide assemblies to small class visits, culminating in a virtual co-presentation with some of the Fessenden High School alums I had met in Florida. I anticipated minor obstacles and significant levels of dissonance. I knew conversations would manifest differently across age and, indeed, race. However, I wanted to speak mostly with Black graduates and former students. I wondered if learning about this history would change things for them. I hoped it would be for everyone, but if I understood race, it had to mean something more to them.

There were many highs and lows, some major, but all noteworthy because I was learning along with the school. There was a low point during a sixth-grade class visit when the group seemed to miss the point. Despite my emphasis on the importance of independent Black education, they could not see past the triumphs of the Fessenden family. One youngster stood to salute the images of Frederick and Ferdinand as the class was dismissed, and the others followed by mocking his gesture. The one Black student present made eye contact with me, then looked away, and I knew I had come up short that day.

There was a high point when, after consulting with several Lower School teachers, we finalized a Fessenden Academy reading book for our youngest learners. I could now read the story of the first Fessenden school to kindergarten classes. There was a low point when the turnout to a special parent presentation explaining our efforts to teach this important history in all grades failed to get more than a dozen families. There was a high point when an eighth-grade boy stayed after my talk to shake my hand and say thank you. There was a low point when writer's block ensued, and I reached research burnout. There was a high point when I received a vote of confidence and encouragement from several of Frederick's grandchildren and great-grandchildren, many of whom had grown up at the school. There was a low point when my proposal to the National Association of Independent Schools was denied. There was a high point when a parent shared that they were on vacation in Florida, and their first-grader recalled the Fessenden Academy story. There was a low point when the most active cohort of Black alums canceled an opportunity to hear the full story, and we never rescheduled. There was a high point when one of those Black alums, a faculty member and colleague at Fessenden, and a former student of mine at Exeter, Warren Charleston, inspired the title of this work when he shared, "I have a new pride about being from

Fessenden." And there was a low point when I learned that I likely missed the chance to speak with Craig Lovell.

In the winter of 2023, I decided to expand my outreach to include Craig's family members, and a relative responded with the sobering news that Craig had passed away the previous summer. This was a definitive low. Amidst a season of personal loss, grieving came naturally. I experienced a wide range of emotions and stopped researching and writing for several weeks. There were so many unanswered questions, but I had no choice but to accept the lack of closure. Still, I wondered if the school could acknowledge his passing in some way, but with what context, and would that be his desire or that of his loved ones? I tried to answer these questions myself before alerting my colleagues to the sad news. Our collective wisdom didn't produce much of a resolution; it did unearth the missing details about Craig's time at Fessenden.

Reading the correspondence between Hart and the Lovell family without the perspective of a first-hand witness or second-hand memory to corroborate the details felt like a breach, not of trust, for they are historical artifacts, but a breach of silence. Muted voices cannot relay memory in the same way that an incurious mind will not question. We knew Craig had entered Fessenden in the fall of 1957 and had left by the spring of 1960 for unnamed reasons. From the beginning, I had assumptions about why, but I had no conclusive evidence. The news of Craig's passing rattled me—what if I had started questioning, researching, and connecting the dots earlier? It also produced the final letter between the school and Craig's family.

Dr. Lovell writes, "I regret that Craig will not be returning to Fessenden this year. I realize that this information is reaching you quite late, especially when I stated earlier that he would be continuing. I did not decide until a few days ago when Craig returned from camp and I had a final chat with him." In the following paragraphs, Dr. Lovell explains that Craig missed being with more familiar friends and that he had become unhappy at school. In particular, his new peers had made him quite aware of his ethnic difference from time to time. The letter continues, "I reasoned these matters out with Craig very carefully on several occasions and tried to get over to him the immense opportunities which the school offered…if anything, his convictions seemed to be stronger that he did not wish to return to Fessenden but rather to go to junior high school in Wellesley." Dr. Lovell concluded his letter with a final paragraph expressing reverence and gratitude to the entire Fessenden faculty. He signed the letter, and with that, the brief tenure of Fessenden's first Black student came to a close.

As a father, I know that a letter could never capture the raw deliberation that must have occurred at home, but I could not shake the question: What exactly did Craig see and hear? Young children are less likely than adults to observe or remember subtle mistreatment. But children remember overt acts. Pain and discomfort are extreme motivators. Most of us do not need a second bee sting to learn the lesson. I was consumed by the irony of what was at stake for the Lovells then and what I observe in schools today. I have read this email before. I have had this same conversation with Black parents, I have had this same conversation in my living room, and, after sixty years, the material obstacles of educating a Black child have shifted only so slightly.

Hart Fessenden responded to the letter as one might expect from a head of school. He was professional in his word choice, staunch in his defense of the school, and regretful to hear of Craig's unhappiness. Hart noted that Craig's joyfulness had been missing for some time, and he did not deny the alleged racism. He wrote, "I'll add that I was extremely concerned to read that Craig had been teased by the boys. I was unaware of any more than one or two episodes, and they, I thought, were of an entirely passing nature. I regret exceedingly that in the boy's eyes this wasn't the case." He concluded his letter with an important note: "He is a fine boy, an able boy, and because of that it is doubly incumbent upon you to, in one way or another, manage to make Craig again serene and happy. I certainly hope you succeed, not only for the boy's sake but for the whole larger matter of race relations."

I tried to place myself in Hart's 1960 worldview. What did he mean to suggest about the larger matter of race relations? Was the irony not apparent? I then tried to imagine being the recipient, but my feelings were too strong. I cannot speak for Dr. Lovell or Craig, but my mind paced through a litany of questions that had no definitive answers. In time, I resolved this open-endedness with a quote from Zora Neale Hurston: "If you are silent about your pain, they will kill you and say you enjoyed it."[109] I have shared this quote with Black prep school students before, and it felt appropriate once again. It may seem extreme, and inevitably, some will miss the point; yet, for my students, what is understood needs no explanation. I take comfort in knowing that father and son did eventually voice their pain. And, any remaining thoughts or doubts I held found a home in the wisdom offered by writer Neely Fuller: "If you do not understand white supremacy and racism, what it is, and how it works, everything else you think you understand will only confuse you."[110]

American schools, both public and private, have educated generations of leading men who understood a particular function of school, the world, and race. This is not to suggest a monolith, nor to offer an excuse. Instead, it is important to recognize that the ways in which this nation functions depend on the lessons these men learn as boys. By the 1960s, those functions faced an organized demand for change. If there was any confusion about what the absence of Black people in an American school, public or private, implied, then one does not understand racism, what it is, or how it works.

In a speech to the Massachusetts State Legislature, Dr. Martin Luther King Jr. proclaimed, "Now is the time to end segregation in public schools."[111] The year was 1965, and by April, the world had seen the assassination of Malcolm X, the escalation of fighting in South Vietnam, and in Boston, the brewing of racial hostilities. Only a month prior, in the face of violent intolerance and committed segregationists, Dr. King helped lead the march from Selma to Montgomery. However, in Boston, between 1964 and 1965, the local civil rights struggle centered on access to quality education. Community activists sought to end racial segregation and the underfunding of Boston's public schools. Legal segregation, or de jure segregation, was deemed unconstitutional in the 1954 U.S. Supreme Court decision Brown v. Board of Education. But in the decade that followed, access to quality education for many Black children, including those in Boston, saw slight improvement. Opponents of reform claimed that racial disparities were the result of housing, and the homogeneity of neighborhoods, which they sought to maintain, amounted to a de facto segregation and, therefore, was not unconstitutional. Dr. King saw it differently. "In a real sense," he stated, "segregation, whether it is de jure segregation of certain sections of the South or de facto segregation of the North, is a new form of slavery covered up with certain niceties of complexities. And all men of goodwill all over this nation must work together passionately and unrelentingly to solve this problem."[112]

Dr. King did not speak directly about private schools. He focused his efforts on the systems oppressing the majority of Black Americans. If segregation defined the debate around public education during the 1960s, then exclusivity, wealth barriers, intelligence testing, and racial bias defined the nature of private education. Public schools and the local governments that controlled them could no longer trample upon civil and human rights without a response from organized Black folk, but for private schools, changes had to come from within. Dr. King spent his life preaching to the soul of America, attempting to compel the government and the public sector to operate without racial prejudice and to invest in the good of the people over that of corporations or private interests. It is hard to imagine exactly what Dr. King would've said to young Black children integrating white private schools. He was a product of Black schools, Black religion, and Black teachers. I believe he would have cautioned Black parents. Still, for the Fessenden School, it would take the reality of the world losing Dr. King's voice before the next Black student would enroll.

As it was made clear, Craig Lovell was Fessenden's first Black student, but not its first Black graduate. That honor belonged to Stuart Perry, who was proud of the distinction. He shared this important pretext when we spoke during the winter of 2023. "The thing about Fessenden was that after the assassination of Dr. King, there was a lot of opportunity for Black people that opened up," Perry recalled. "There was affirmative action in employment; I think my father was a beneficiary of that. Also, as a result of that, a lot of Black kids, like myself, got full scholarships to private schools that they never would have had the opportunity to attend. At least not like that. Just about all my friends had scholarships to private schools across the country. Some of them went to Noble and Greenough, some of them went to Lawrence Academy, and there was Cushing Academy. And, we had a network; the Black students kept in touch. We had Black student unions, but that came much later, but it wasn't at Fessenden when I was there."

Hart Fessenden's tenure as headmaster ended in the spring of 1967, and while Fessenden family members helped guide the school from the trustee level, they no longer managed daily operations. In the eight years between Craig Lovell's withdrawal and Stuart Perry's arrival, thirty-four African nations and several Caribbean nations claimed independence from European colonizers; the U.S. Congress passed the Civil Rights Act of 1964 and the Voting Rights Act of 1965, and Black Power was born. A global struggle against white supremacist ideology and imperialism marked this period. 1968 was a particularly tumultuous year. Still, there's no clear indication in the Fessenden records suggesting that the leadership enacted a new policy to attract Black students. It was not exactly explicit to Perry, either. "It was something that I found out later, and as I said, most of the Black kids that I knew in my age group, within two to three years older and younger, went to private schools. The girls went to places like Dana Hall and Newton Country Day. I know that Dr. King's assassination was still in the air when I came to Fessenden because that's how a lot of the students approached me. They begin with telling me what they knew about Dr. King. They also would tell me that I looked like Sydney Poitier, but I didn't. But that was the only frame of reference they had as far as a Black person. I either looked like Sydney Poitier or Bill Cosby because that's all they knew. Conversations about the assassination definitely went on during my freshman year. Dr. King and Robert Kennedy were killed within a few months of each other, so tension filled the air. And then there was Vietnam."

Perry was excited to learn how Fessenden had progressed since his time, and he was especially intrigued by the Fessenden Academy in Florida. We spoke on the phone several times before he agreed to share his Fessenden story with me. I was especially keen to learn how the adults in his life cultivated a sense of Black pride before, during, and after his years at Fessenden. His father attended the 1963 March on Washington for Jobs and Freedom, headlined by Dr. King's *I Have a Dream* speech.

Well, my mother and father were very progressive Black people. They were engaged with the Black community in education pursuits, supporting the city council and the politics of the area. My mother taught African-American studies at Mount Ida College in Newton. She also taught early childhood development there for almost thirty-five years. My father was a banker, so I was steeped in Black history, and I had a lot of Black pride well before I came to Fessenden, which was the fall of 1968, when I was 11 years old.

Perry continued:

I was the beneficiary of a full scholarship, and I remember visiting during the summer of 1968. I remember my parents brought me to this school, this big place, and I took a test with this lady named Miss McElvoy. She was about ninety years old and it turned out that she had been with the school since about the time that my dad was born in 1934 or 1935. And she gave me all these tests like math and writing, and she asked me some Shakespeare. I think I really impressed her because I had just read *The Tempest* by Shakespeare before I took that test. So when she asked me if I knew anything Shakespeare wrote, I said *The Tempest*. So I aced that, and I think I kind of surprised her.

If there was a policy to enroll local Black youth in the fall of 1968, it seems to have been reactionary and ad hoc. As Perry remembers:

I took that test, and we left, and I forgot all about it. I started my regular school, my public school, and I was in school for what I think might have been two weeks. And I came home from school one day, and my father and mother told me to pack my clothes and I would be going to boarding school across town, and I had forgotten completely about that. I didn't have any idea that I was going to be living there, you know. It was like I came home from school, and they told me that. And later that night I was there.

Today, we refer to it as culture shock when students experience difficulty adjusting to a drastically unfamiliar environment. All schools are vested in the early success of the students they admit. However, the nature of private schools alters the calculus. The cost of tuition per pupil is directly tied to the school's operating budget, which means scholarships are private philanthropic investments. As much as The Fessenden School may have wanted to open its doors to Black students, the bill would be paid by individual progenitors who wanted to see a change. It has often been repeated that some white parents grew tolerant of Black students in order to prepare their children for a changing world. It is certainly true that forward thinking white parents with resources can create a progressive enclave as they define it. Schools unlike any other sector of American life allow for an intimate generational rejection of prejudice. And this has an appeal. However, it does nothing to prevent the harmful impact of racial bias. It's important to recognize that the shocking culture Black students entered was informed by well-wishers, naysayers, advocates, fair-weather fans, people with bigoted ideas, justice lovers, and those on the fence about change. It was far from a monolith. Non-Black peers absorb these mentalities from the adults in their lives, and Black students must learn to navigate those unfiltered encounters. Faculty carry even more complexity to their work; with discretionary decision-making built into the job, Black students' learning and well-being were at the mercy of their teachers, dorm parents, and coaches.

"It was very, very regimented and very conservative. I'm sure it still is. But I mean, I'm talking about 1968," Perry continued. "The school had the same mindset and values from the days of the founders. There were faculty who had been there since the 1930s. And when you're aware of that, and you see pictures of them hanging in the halls, you realize they've lived most of their lives at Fessenden. Teaching and raising their families." Perry paused to ask if this was true today, and I assured him that the model of residential teaching faculty hadn't changed much. "But as I was saying, it was very conservative. Everything was yes sir, no sir. We had to stand when a woman came to the table; we had to take turns waiting in the dining room. That was not a bad thing. At the time, you think it's drudgery, but I mean, in the scheme of things, it was not a bad thing. It taught you early on that at some time in your life, you will have to do service. And if you're going to be of service, you might as well learn to do it well."

"And there was another Black kid my age who came in with me. His name was Cornel Ratlift, and he was a five-day boarder, too. All things considered, for that time period, I know I was a curiosity initially. But I don't recall having anything bad racially happening to me. I know it's been fifty-some-odd years, but I think I would remember something like that. I remember, you know, kids playing around. I played around, too. But I don't ever remember anything really malicious, racially."

Perry entered as a seventh grader in 1968 and graduated, as is tradition for Fessenden, after his ninth-grade year in 1971. One or two more Black boys would enroll in the succeeding years, but Perry was the single Black graduate in 1971. Reflecting on his time at Fessenden, I see that his positive memories outweigh any challenges he experienced. "What stands out is that I learned my study habits from Fessenden. I learned how to study well and to prioritize my time. I learned how to prepare for class, a test, or give a presentation. Before Fessenden, I knew I had to do my homework, but they did a good job inculcating in you a desire to learn."

Perry continued:

They made you participate in things you might not ordinarily do. For example, every kid had to do a sport. I didn't mind that, but to be honest, Fessenden was my very first experience with

134

organized sports. And, because I was there for a few years, I realized what my true skills were. But it was good that they made you go out for a sport. Everyone had to participate in some kind of extracurricular activity as well. I played junior varsity baseball, basketball, and football and enjoyed my time in the Glee Club and the Drama Club. I wasn't outstanding, but I wasn't bad. This sort of stuff should be in archives as well as that column I told you about. Did you find my story about Nat Turner?

The Albemarle is a Fessenden School publication that dates back to the school's initial years. By the 1920s, the part-literary magazine, part-student news bulletin printed each semester, had an editorial board, and was popular among students, their families, and the faculty. Additionally, *The Albemarle* was exchanged nationwide and abroad with similar publications from more than sixty other prestigious schools, including Horace Mann School for Boys in New York City; The Shipley School in Bryn Mawr, Pennsylvania; Browne and Nichols School in Cambridge, Massachusetts; Roxbury Latin School in West Roxbury, Massachusetts; Polytechnic School in Pasadena, California; Chicago Latin School in Chicago, Illinois; Ecole de Garcons, Jules Ferry in Sanvic, France; and George Watson's College in Edinburgh, Scotland. Perry's 1968 poem about Nat Turner had an untold readership in the most exclusive environments of his era.

I asked Perry, "Why Nat Turner? Can you remember why you decided to write about the most racially polarizing figure in your first year at a new school? And how did everyone react?" He responded:

My first exposure to Nat Turner's story was in 1964 when my uncle Donald presented me with a book titled *A Pictorial History of the Negro in America*, edited by Langston Hughes. I was seven years old and just beginning to appreciate my love of books. In particular, books on Black American History. Nat Turner was one of several people profiled, and I had never heard of him before. And the idea that an enslaved person would revolt against his oppressors was absolutely foreign to my mindset. And with violence! Of course, he had to meet his demise. And they had to make an example of his death, so it was terrible. An engraving from one of the old news magazines or weeklies from that era showed Nat Turner being captured. He looked strong and defiant and had a sword on his hip. Then, around the time that I started going to Fessenden School, a book about Nat Turner by William Styron came out. It was more of a fictionalized story about Nat Turner. Martin Luther King had just been assassinated. I was a little leery of his non-violent program to get things done and became more inclined towards people like Muhammad Ali, Jim Brown, and some of the more militant young guns.

Perry's feelings as a seventh-grade student were in line with those of many Black Americans following King's assassination. Exclamations of grief turned destructive at times, and the show of force from militarized police did little to calm the anguish. In hundreds of U.S. cities, violence erupted, and thousands of federal troops were called into mostly Black neighborhoods across the country to suppress outrage. Boston's Roxbury neighborhood was already lacerating from police encounters and the rioting of the summer of 1967. Images of a city on fire were perhaps only averted when Black community leaders convinced Boston city officials to allow James Brown, Soul Brother Number

One, to perform a televised concert just twenty-four hours after King's murder. But reactions varied. Stokely Carmichael passionately declared, "When white America killed Dr. King last night, she declared war on us." By the fall of 1968, when Perry entered Fessenden, there was no collective healing in sight, and the wounds of Black Americans were still open and throbbing. The murder of the nation's most prominent Civil Rights leader broke through the bubble of New England private schooling in a way that King's living, his words, and his ideas never did.

In March of 1968, three weeks before his assassination, security was on high alert in Grosse Point, Michigan, when Dr. King delivered his *The Other America* speech to a predominantly white crowd at a local high school. A few Black attendees were scattered throughout the room; however, from King's rhetoric that night, it was clear that his target audience was predominantly middle- and upper-class white Americans. There were credible concerns for King's safety that night. White mob violence and extrajudicial activity are as old as the nation, and Dr. King's critique of the Vietnam War gave cover for his detractors to unite against his visit. Entering with the local chief of police personally shielding him, Dr. King delivered his remarks despite protests and disruptions. He painted a candid picture of inequality in the United States. Directly naming the country's racism and explaining how white people, white institutions, white communities, white society, and white suburbs maintain the experience of two Americas. Midway through Dr. King's speech, we get a foreshadowing, "And I must say tonight that a riot is the language of the unheard. And what is it America has failed to hear? It has failed to hear that the plight of the negro poor has worsened over the last twelve or fifteen years. It has failed to hear that the promises of freedom and justice have not been met. And it has failed to hear that large segments of white society are more concerned about tranquility and the status quo than about justice and humanity."

The same must be asked on a local level. What did the Fessenden School fail to hear or see? Much like its peer schools, metaphorically, Fessenden was part of a chain of educational islands. Removed from the circumstances facing most school-age children, the desire was for distraction-free teaching and learning. While it is understandable for a private boarding school to strive for this ideal, it isn't exactly attainable. None of us lives in a vacuum. Instead, this inward reflection often limits the perspective students encounter when their minds are most malleable. Concurrently, to serve a particular profile of students extremely well, adults are asked to fit within a set of homogeneous beliefs that often lead to underdeveloped pedagogical skills. In such settings, racial and class divisions leave little room for diverse opinions shaped by diverse experiences. To be clear, this is how most families want it. Intellectual challenges to the dominant perspective can be celebrated, but material demands are a different matter altogether. It is a privilege either way; it is also supply-demand economics. The curriculum always reflects consciousness, consumers have choice, and those choices set a market standard.

I can not imagine what it must have felt like to teach and learn at the Fessenden School between 1968 and 1971, but I recall living out the Black Lives Matter movement on the campuses of prestigious private schools. I recall the murders of unarmed Black people. I recall the acquittals. I recall my helplessness the most. I recall explaining to a room full of other people's children why it is that police can kill with impunity. I recall being asked why the deceased could not comply, where is this structural racism you speak of, why would they burn down their own community, and what can I do as a teenager? I recall sharing Dr. King's words. I recall trying to convince administrators, career educators, and students that classes and assignments could wait, only to discover that they actually could not wait. I recall my decision to stop making excuses for colleagues and school policy. I recall struggling to distinguish between untrained, colorblind, white-adjacent, corporate ladder-climbers and the morally-conflicted but silent colleague from the racist type. I recall how excited most were to get things back to normal. I recall being unheard. I recall trying to make sense of why the hell I was there. I recall feeling alone in a sea of whiteness, and, like Perry, I decided to bring my ancestors and memory to school with me.

"I also think that I may have wanted to write something, perhaps a little bit shocking, as a way of introducing myself to the Fessenden community," Perry concluded. Unbeknownst to him at the time, his reputation as an outspoken Black man was widespread among the Fessenden faculty. One teacher cited Perry for saying, "I'm not going to take orders from a white woman." Another teacher commented, "His flashes of uncooperativeness and the like are manifestations that he must take a position on the civil rights issue." A different teacher offered, "In some ways, Stuart is a microcosm of the difficulties which a Negro in our society experiences in trying to discover who he is. Through writing, reading, and acting, Stuart has found constructive ways to relieve his frustrations. Stuart is sensitive, so sensitive that he detects hypocrisies that adults live…. Stuart has a strong basic knowledge of what's right and wrong." A similar impression was left among the student body. The Class Prophecy is a satirical essay written by students to predict the lives of all graduating seniors. Perry is referenced as a future Black militant.

Truthfully, Perry was a budding artist and is more fondly remembered for his stage performances, joyful spirit, and charisma. After Fessenden, he attended Lawrence Academy for one year before making the difficult decision to return home to complete his high school education. With college already in his sights, Perry reasoned that three more years in a culturally non-affirming school was not in his best interest. More than anything, he wanted to be with his family. But what if a parallel learning environment infused with Black scholarship, uplift, and heritage, and removed from the gaze of whiteness, was available? Perhaps there might be room for extended family, truth, and service. It was of no surprise to me that Perry went on to become a theater major at the illustrious Howard University. Popularly known to Howard students as The Mecca, Howard University is to Black elites what Fessenden, Exeter, and Harvard are to their white counterparts.

There are models for how to be Black at a private school, and disarming white people is definitely the safest approach. Times have changed, and so too has the landscape of Black families interested in private schools. It is clear that Black families electing for a privatized education for their children have done so with great intentionality. These families, and ideally, their ambitious students, have a plan: how to market themselves, which sports to play, how many world languages to study, what to read, what career aspirations to pursue, what contributions to make to the school community, and what to accomplish with this tremendous opportunity. The list goes on. Years of preparation and coaching on how to show up—and by that, I mean how to make white people comfortable and how to impress independent schools with your exceptionalism—is fairly common.

As a strategy, I have little critique. It is a historically valid approach that we learn from our predecessors. Joseph Wiley belonged to a generation of Black educators in the first half of the twentieth century who understood the skill of disarming white people very clearly and taught it to their students. The generation of Black children and college students who integrated segregated public schools and universities during the 1960s and beyond have documented the vile treatment they endured and taught us how to survive those environments. Wherever we find progress in schools today, it is largely due to this continuum. But there will come a time when this current generation of Black students must decide whether to bring their memories with them. If parents and early teachers have not equipped them with memory and racial pride, then this inheritance will be lost. But if they can somehow reach back, remember, and bring it forward, discomfort along with resilience surely awaits them. It remains to be seen who will stand with them.

****

At one extreme, I often wonder if there is a difference between the Black child attending a public school named after a Confederate general and the Black child walking the campus of a private school built on usurped Native lands and funded in part by wealth taken from their ancestors. I often wonder if Black students in the Deep South experience being called nigger as frequently as Black students in New England prep schools. As appalling as it may seem, the most exclusive rooms tend to have

141

the most offensive language. It is an unspoken reality that wealth often buys cover for immoral behavior, and schools are certainly not exempt from this. The n-word becomes the litmus test for racism, so students learn not to get caught. Meanwhile, self-appointed progressive educators are quick to tell me that every identity group has an n-word. On this extreme, everyone is an ally, and Black students are rendered as a signal of progress. In such environments, students are sooner to learn Black History taught as a figment of mainstream white imagination or the politics of white liberalism than they are to have actual Black teachers.

Perry ended our conversation with a critical thought: "In the scheme of things, even when you told me about being maybe the first, it's not really all that important to me. But if it's useful to somebody, or if you need to have a starting point, you know. Then. I am honored by that. It really gives me a good feeling to know that you are working on a project like this, because I didn't have any Black teachers at Fessenden. The students must be really fortunate to have a teacher like yourself." As I graciously received his compliment, I knew all too well the power and limitations of representation. Whatever I can positively contribute to the lives of Black school children is a duty I owe them—a duty that transcends work obligations, an ethos of which I am a beneficiary, and an ethic that I sincerely plan to uphold.

Educators versed in the language of Diversity, Equity, and Inclusion (DEI) will be familiar with the curricular concept of windows and mirrors. A window describes a learning opportunity for students to see perspectives and identities different from their own. For Black students at Fessenden, everything and everyone is a window, which is why they master the art of code-switching so effectively. At the same time, Black students are representatives of the race; the benefit of being an individual does not really exist. The stakes remain high as they are typically the single window through which students and adults discover differences and learn racial tolerance. And, lest I forget, Black students are children.

Conversely, those in the statistical majority experience school made in their very image, not only among peers and teaching faculty, but also in the school's branding, its hung portraits, and its curriculum. All are mirrors, reinforcing belonging. There is mentorship and empathy for those students by default. Most substantially, having mirrors in what you learn and who teaches it allows self-pride to blossom organically. This rooting of identity and purpose illuminates a pathway for young people far beyond grade school. For Black children, they enter upon a literal hall of mirrors. Disorienting but manageable at best. Damaging and inescapable at worst. Diversity recruitment, equity statements, and inclusion programs are not designed to address this issue structurally, despite the notable improvements they bring. When schools place more emphasis on eliminating the presence of racial slurs like the n-word than they do on correcting the absence of Black adults, Black alumni, and an intergenerational Black community, then schools haven't learned the lesson offered by their Black students.

I have accepted some harsh realities for myself. As a father, I have had to forgive myself often because I could not shield my own two children from the racism of private schools. As a faculty member, I have a hard time making sense of why I could not protect Black children from the educational malpractice of colleagues. As a school administrator, I regret to admit that I simply cannot professionally develop a sense of consciousness. Black educators in independent schools tend to be isolated from an intergenerational Black community, much like their students. Some are true believers. They have witnessed enough good and felt enough kindness to allow them to believe in the mission of their school. Some are naive and do not know what they do not know. Some have calculated risk versus reward and have determined that the means justify the ends. Others are so well adjusted to whiteness or their own privilege that there is no second thought, let alone time for memory. Most will say, "I am here for the children." Many people feel trapped due to economic constraints. To a degree, I have been each of these. But I will never understand those Black teachers who want the job and not the duty. This is where I distinguish between color, culture, and commitment. Thankfully, my predecessors at Fessenden shared in this pursuit to defend Black boys and their Blackness.

Between 1971, when Perry became the first Black graduate at Fessenden, and 1993, seventeen Black boys followed him without the consistent care of Black classroom teachers or administrators. They are men of distinction today, but as children, their families discovered Fessenden in their own way. With different origin stories, their Blackness wasn't well defined nor necessarily salient in the same way for each of them. Blackness was then, and has historically been, constructed in opposition to those perceived as white. One needs to be told what their skin color means and then experience it before they believe it. By the 1960s, resistance to a three-hundred-and-fifty-year history of degradation and stigma led to expressions of Black Pride as we know it today. But this, too, must be taught. Otherwise, a learned self-hatred can metastasize. Ranging in color, ethnicity, and socioeconomic status, these young men of Fessenden comprised local boys who earned scholarships, as well as others from the African and Caribbean diaspora, including those of wealth and royalty.

Today, you are less likely to find Black students who descend from the enslaved Africans brought to North America in the most selective colleges and private schools. The net impact of this is at least twofold. Independent schools and universities can more easily ignore the narrative of the enslaved and the children of Jim Crow segregation in their pursuit of multiculturalism. Black, African, and African American are multiracial and multiethnic-inclusive terms, and as schools commit to a financially solvent model of recruiting Black students who can add socioeconomic diversity, i.e., full-pay Black students, the shared experience may exist in name only. With the moral scale of these decisions unbalanced as it is, a fiscally sound position masks a weak attempt at breaking a racial trope that posits Black students earn admittance without merit and enroll because of financial aid. Indeed, academic institutions could simply teach better. Racial tropes are learned. Exposing students to the origins of American schooling and wealth creation in a way that dissolves racial bias and intellectual supremacy is a sound curriculum and a choice often ignored. Instead, the most likely outcome is a depoliticization of Blackness. Those with the strongest claim for reparation against the American educational system are likely to be outnumbered, certainly on campus, but even in their own affinity spaces. These are the decisions of schools that care not to see the trees among the forest, let alone the connectivity of the roots. Whereas for students and their families, appreciating what makes each of us uniquely Black and inextricably linked together and to Africa is a lesson often dropped in pursuit of acquiring more disarming traits.

An oral history confirmed by Dan Kiley, who joined the faculty in 1982 and served as Head of School, Assistant Head of School, and Head of Middle School during his illustrious career, suggests that Wayne Owens was the first Black teacher hired by The Fessenden School. Arriving in 1981, Owens does not appear in the official record because he did not complete the school year. At the time, there were at most four Black students enrolled, so it is hard to determine the scale of his impact. Without Dan Kiley's living memory, the institutional memory as it relates to Black faculty would be incomplete. However, it is clear that in 1993, when Robert Greene joined the Fessenden faculty as a mathematics teacher, coach, and member of the residential team, he became the first Black teacher to complete a tenure.

Greene and I first met at Exeter during a tumultuous time for one of the world's most noteworthy secondary schools. Our love for mathematics was not what brought us together. Rather, during the spring semester of 2017, student activism on Exeter's campus reached a historic climax as Black and Latinx students documented their experiences with racism on film and spontaneously organized what was later reported as a sit-in of the principal's office. The school then hired Greene as a DEI consultant, and he worked with the principal's leadership team and the board of trustees. As the newest member of the Exeter leadership team and only a few months removed from the classroom, Greene was an elder statesman in my eyes. I went from the sidelines of advising student groups to advising the top brass, which required tactful navigation. Greene and I connected as Black male educators, positioned with our own credentials and accomplishments, but more specifically, in that moment, because Black students and those who stood with them dared to operate with agency.

The duty of a Black educator is never far from one's mind when considering a job. Greene, a native southerner who calls Atlanta home, is a son and grandson of teachers. He spent his undergraduate years in Providence, Rhode Island, but his reasons for seeking employment were as much about his heritage as a matter of practicality:

I was familiar with New England, and my experience as an undergraduate teaching and research assistant had cemented my interest in a teaching career, so those were the positions I had looked for. I had not gone through any kind of certification track for public school when I was an undergrad, so I thought my best pathways were independent schools. At the time, there was an organization in Boston called Channels for Educational Choices. It was one of the precursors for access and opportunity for teachers of color, particularly Black teachers, and they had a job fair. Many of the schools were offering internships. I was like, no, I need more money than that. I need a job. Fessenden offered a job. And it had housing.

Greene continued, "I can remember in particular thinking about taking the job. I thought, 'There are only two Black students in the upper school, one in ninth grade, and another in seventh grade.' And then I thought, you know, quite honestly, because there are only two, there's still a need. I felt called to go to the school. Even if there were only one brother there, he would get my best. In many ways, I felt called because it certainly wasn't the demographics." In Greene's deliberations, he knew he could do the job and maintain a strong sense of community despite the relative isolation. He knew he would have the support and brotherhood of his local fraternity chapter if he chose to join the all-white faculty at Fessenden. As a member of Omega Psi Phi, a Black Greek letter organization founded in 1911 at Howard University on the principles of manhood, scholarship, perseverance, and uplift, Greene experienced the power of affinity in a non-affirming learning environment. However, racial fraternity was not an option for this generation of Fessenden boys, but perhaps mentorship would be.

As Greene recalled, "I felt that I owed them, because that was me paying it forward. I'm standing on the shoulders of my ancestral giants. So it was very true for me, because it's a part of our heritage. We've got a collectivist culture and mindset, and we believe in bringing the whole community along. And so, I carried that with me when I arrived at the school." He continued,

It was also really interesting to see the personality that the boys had taken on because there weren't a lot of black students with them, and even fewer black role models or adults who were around.... My perception was that they were kind of buffeted about by the stereotypes that their peers held of them. They kind of leaned into those stereotypes because they didn't have anything else to hold on to that they could anchor themselves against.... In general, we would talk about being a black male in America, being a black male at Fessenden, and what it meant, where they would go with their questions, their wonderings, and how they were trying to develop a self-identity. What was possible for them, and what provisions they had to resist the cultural tides that tried to circumscribe them. I think that may have been the most empowering outcome. They didn't have to be circumscribed by anybody else's definition.

Between the job and the duty, there is another important responsibility for Black teachers in white spaces: the burden. It is an uncompensated part of the role, definitely unwritten in any official manner, but unquestionably necessary, a labor that is not for us or about us, and one with limited reciprocity. The burden is an additional demand, regardless of one's field of expertise, to explain race, to humanize Black people, and to be the shining counter-narrative to racial stereotypes. The burden is relatively light when teaching young people, but it is a heavy decision when it comes to adults. Offering critique and guidance to school leadership, or providing feedback to colleagues and parents, comes at a personal cost, but allowing harm to continue is personally regrettable. As Greene shared, "I also felt that my presence was important for the white students because they were the dominant demographic, as well as for their families and other students of color. We had many more students of Asian, South East Asian, and Latino heritage than we did Black and African American students at the time."

Greene would be the first Black coworker for some faculty and the first Black teacher for many students. Boys from across the country and the world had come to Fessenden, expecting to see a white man lead a classroom. Adults may have gone decades without needing to check their rhetoric or biases. It cannot be overlooked nor overstated that for non-Black students and their families, a Black school teacher is usually the first, and, too often, the last Black authority figure of consequence in their lives. Few adults shape a young person's worldview like a teacher can. Nestled in a classroom, the teacher is the single adult who grants permission, serves as a daily moral compass, offers encouragement, intervenes when harm occurs, provides incentives, rewards, and general feedback, and authors the official record for a student. It is a powerful deconstruction when the adult responsible for this care does so in a skin for which the world, as most know it, has shown no value.

Greene likely sparked some cognitive dissonance in students' minds when they discovered he was a math instructor. The same incongruence that stares down on Black students stares up towards Black teachers. But students are rarely the problem. The classroom is sacred, and young people learn to admire caregivers of any race. The main reason why Black teachers feel unwelcome or eventually leave their schools is the racist treatment they experience from colleagues, school leaders, and adults close to the school. So, along with the job, and the duty, and the burden, there is the fight.

The fight is self-advocacy at its core. It is a defensive posture to shield oneself or students from repeated trauma and the onslaught of micro- and macro-aggressions. Sometimes, it is as simple as basic courtesy or a longing to be seen. It is never because of one incident. Black teachers often strive against a pattern of behavior, and in most cases, their efforts are corrective or aimed at easing the path for others. The fight is a stance against overt acts, whereas the burden is a preemptive battle, a vaccine, and an antibiotic for the disease of racist educational environments. The only thing more draining than teaching people how not to be racist is fighting with those who think they do not need the lesson. Of course, none of this will appear in a job description, and for the longest time, schools considered strong advocates of Black students and teachers to be adversarial.

Far from the proper compensation they deserve, Black teachers risk isolation from colleagues, a falling glass ceiling on their careers, being typecast, and termination. A good fight looks like an intergenerational relay—it needs to be modeled—but when you are the only, as it was for Greene, you embody the fight, you carry the burden, and you are duty-bound.

Greene spent two years at Fessenden before pursuing a graduate degree at Harvard University's Graduate School of Education. The timing was not great for the boys or the school, but the opportunity to deepen his craft was too much to pass up. Greene left the school as a beloved faculty member and colleague. Even today, some thirty years later, fondness for the people he met remains. To honor his impact, graduating ninth graders offered a dedication which, in part, reads:

The Class of 1994 proudly dedicates this yearbook to Mr. Robert Greene. He is a great coach, a great influence, and everybody respects him. He tells you what you do well, and makes you a better all around athlete. He makes the whole team build character. He teaches us not only about math but about all cultures, subjects and life in general. He always listens to your problems. He has made a big difference in educating the entire Upper School in ethnic differences and holidays. He is a wonderful math teacher and he recognizes extra effort and talent on the part of his students.

One final remark stands out to me. Greene recalls when he unofficially learned that he was the first. "Before the year begins, there's a dinner mixer with trustees and faculty. And, I can remember the chair of the board of trustees, at the time, approaching me at that event. You know, kind of clapping me on the back, and he said, 'Hey, you know, we're so glad we're breaking that color line.' And I thought, first of all, did he just say that? I couldn't believe he said it like that. So I had to pause and say to myself, okay, this actually feels familiar. So I told him, 'You know I quite honestly don't mind being the first. But I don't expect to be the last, not even next year, I don't expect to be the only. So I'm looking at you to do something about that.' I essentially throw it back with all the confidence of youth."

It would take some years, but with the leadership of several key administrators, Fessenden began to recruit and retain a more diverse faculty. For a brief window of time during the 1994–1995 school year, a history teacher would be the first to succeed Greene. Then, in 1998, Damon Carter would embark upon a seven-year tenure teaching in the Music Department and working with the school's Admissions Office. In addition to quickly becoming a beloved member of the Fessenden community, Carter ushered in the first iteration of an affinity group. They called it Onyx.

Our understanding of racial affinity groups depends on the frame from which we view them. To be clear, in this context, affinity with whiteness is the norm for which all others contrast. We've seen that explicit exclusion and legal segregation aren't required to create a whites-only, or better said, an only-white school. The former is what we picture when we imagine the conditions of the Deep South. The latter is what we see among so-called elite private schools, universities, and wealthy suburban districts. The only people, programs, and places from which such schools derive a legacy are undeniably white. Even when confronted with a different origin story, most will still seek a bridge to some version of Eurocentricity. The presence of others, as diverse as they may make a space, does little to change these realities.

Affinity groups, as we know them today, originated with student activism in the 1960s. Beverly Daniel Tatum's aptly titled book, *Why Are All the Black Kids Sitting Together in the Cafeteria*, chronicles the psychological need for all students to seek racial affinity. We see a similar longing for affinity with the stories of the first Black students at Fessenden. However, gathering collectively, even for therapeutic purposes, when your presence at school has already been politicized and debated, will cause consternation. In reality, it requires a relay of memory before Black students can appreciate the power of their gathering. The Black Studies movement, which swept across hundreds of U.S. campuses, and the creation of Black Student Unions, are great examples of how comprehensive solutions emerge from establishing community. Within one generation, Black students went from shielding each other from the intolerance of their schools to successfully organizing for policy change.

By the late 1990s, fueled by an expanding global market, Fessenden touted a twenty percent student of color population. Boys representing eighty-four towns in Massachusetts, twenty-seven states, and nineteen countries made for an increasingly diverse campus. However, despite those gains, socioeconomic and racial disparities remained, and Black boys were still among the least represented demographic. Outside of Fessenden, this era is marked by explicit claims from peer institutions about the importance of multiculturalism, and minority student support offices sprang up on campuses across the country. In most cases, student activism, paired with a faculty member willing to carry out their duty and continue the fight, created the conditions for change. In the 2001 school year, Lavette Coney came to embody that change.

As a Boston native, Coney was unfamiliar with the Fessenden name or the school until she returned home after eight years of teaching in Japan. "When I returned to the States, I was looking for a job," she shares. "I was working in a charter school, and I don't know how Carney Sandoe, the faculty placement firm, came to my attention, but I went to their hiring event. Fessenden interviewed me on the spot." The hiring team was impressed and recruited Coney immediately. "Dan Kiley was there, and they introduced me to a couple of other people. We went out to lunch and then to dinner. I remember asking to talk to other faculty members, alums, and students to figure out whether Fessenden would be the place for me." Coney understood something important about Fessenden before she even stepped onto campus. Unlike most teaching jobs, boarding schools are highly immersive and designed to attract *fit* or those *who get it*. A hair out of place, an errant comment, or a personality quirk is enough for a hiring committee to pass on an otherwise qualified candidate. Despite their casual nature, meals with various stakeholders are often an extension of the formal vetting process. Coney was wise in ensuring that the interview was mutual.

"What I found out early was that these schools have unwritten rules. It's like a sink-or-swim mentality and environment. And unless you inquired and observed, you probably wouldn't last long." Coney did just that, and the following fall, she embarked upon a twenty-year career at the school, holding various roles during her tenure. When I joined the faculty in 2020, Coney was one of the first people I met, and we immediately formed a connection. In my heart, I knew she had paved the way for me, and I felt as if I owed her my very best. I recalled my Exeter days, where, despite having allies, resistance to hiring a chief diversity officer lasted for many years. I could only imagine what particular obstacles existed at Fessenden prior to my arrival. Coney created space for me as she had done for her boys. The Black men who had Coney as an advisor during their childhood at Fessenden shared similar testimony—*we owe her everything; she took care of me in ways that I didn't know I needed; I didn't appreciate her until I didn't have her at my next school; Ms. Coney is Queen Mother."*

VOICE is Fessenden's longest-serving official affinity space. "It actually came from students and their parents." Led by Lavette Coney, the group was established by boys of African descent. "Parents and ninth-grade students basically begged me to start a group. They said other schools had it, and they wanted it, and they needed it. I approached the head of the school at the time, who was very open to it. He was very accommodating to teachers and generally supported our efforts. So when I asked him if we could start one, I don't think he understood what an affinity group was, but he said yes because he saw that the students needed it. I was willing to start it, and we initially had no problems. However, after some time, he did get some queries and concerns from white parents who were upset. They actually said things like, 'Why are they having secret meetings in our school without us being there?' So he faced significant pushback, but he still said, 'No, I already allowed her to do it, and she's doing it!'"

Unsurprisingly, many of the adults at Fessenden struggled to articulate why a racial affinity space would be necessary for non-white students. By the early 2000s, affinity groups were common, and evidence supporting their effectiveness was decades old. Nonetheless, independent schools have no choice but to respond when the same students they teach to be independent thinkers advocate and organize. Coney shared, "I didn't have personal experience with affinity groups, and I actually had to do some research. I had to learn up on it. I contacted peer schools that had affinity groups, and the one school I leaned heavily on was Noble and Greenough. They had a robust program. I then contacted the DEI person at Brandeis University, and he helped us shape some things as well. Eventually, a consultant spent a whole Saturday with us. He came to talk about the group, help us organize, and put their ideas together. It mainly came from the students. The boys wrote and signed contracts; they established roles for leadership and group officers."

Coney and the boys were building something that, for some, felt foreign, peculiar, unnecessary, and adversarial. For them, it was natural and needed. "The parents were amazed. Throughout the entire time I was doing it, only two students opted out and didn't want to join the group. And they were free to make that decision. I think in both cases, the parents didn't understand. Their teachers didn't understand." Coney continued, "We aren't taught about racial identity development. We talk about childhood psychology, we talk about educational philosophy, but no one talks about racial identity development and what's there. There's a deep lack of knowledge. No one asks, What do you know about yourself? How do you love yourself?" The boys in VOICE were carrying on a radical tradition without a full understanding. They were resisting in the most honest, compassionate, and respectful way. They were also just being children.

For the school, finding a suitable time and location for the boys to meet was always a challenge, but VOICE and Coney also faced direct opposition from some faculty members. There was simply no convincing some adults that Fessenden was hostile in any way that would require Black boys to need a separate space. For them, separation sounded like segregation, and in their ironic worldview, it was affinity groups and their leaders who were guilty of racism. This entrenched perspective remains common enough even today, despite research to the contrary, despite Coney's fight to establish something lasting, despite the burden she shouldered as the only Black female educator. "When someone stands up in a faculty meeting saying we don't need affinity groups at this school, I would say, 'You have to remember, I didn't start this. It was the students and their parents saying they need it. It comes from them; I'm just here to facilitate.' And that was hard, I was on my own, but I knew it was the right thing to do."

Quantitatively, VOICE meetings comprised less than one percent of the time a boarding student spent at school, as the otherwise statistical minority in almost every room they entered. If a Black student was lucky enough to have another Black peer in the same class or dormitory, it never reached a critical mass. Sports were a potential loophole, but not if you were a Black student interested in hockey, lacrosse, squash, tennis, golf, cross-country running, or crew. Coney shared, "They gave us lunchtime to meet, but we found ways around it. We had evening activities; for example, we had Girl Talk, where women in different career fields or graduate school students spoke, and they answered any questions the boys had. We had doctors of African descent and entrepreneurs who spoke as a panel, and we also used weekends. But we did a lot during lunch as well, and teachers didn't always understand that some topics might take more time. If the boys were late because we had an important conversation, not everyone could appreciate that."

Coney continued, "We used the ten-point program, which was also used at Noble and Greenough. Students were asked to rate their academic, family, and personal lives on a scale of one to ten. And any student rating themselves below a six had to talk about it with the group. I would ask if they needed me to contact a teacher on their behalf or speak with a parent, and I would do whatever they needed from me. I instituted that because I wanted to support them." The ten-point program lives on today with some variation. Well before the language of group therapy and normalizing male vulnerability became popular ideologies, the boys in VOICE had an established practice. Over the years, VOICE boys planned Black History Month programs and met luminaries such as Magic Johnson and Nikki Giovanni. VOICE boys spoke with Dr. John Carlos and met Kareem Abdul Jabbar, among many others. Eventually, with Coney's guidance, the boys created a mission statement in 2004 that is recited at the start of every meeting and followed by a chorus of amen, as if it were a prayer. It is a living testimony to Lavette Coney. It is a relay from a generation of Black boys at Fessenden.

The affinity group, VOICE, is intended for boys who self-identify as Black [e.g. African boys of African descent (Ethiopian, Ghanian, Nigerian, etc.), African American, African Caribbean, Afro-Latin, Cape Verdean, including all those from the diaspora] such that their self-image is shaped by the history of racial discrimination against Black people in the United States and the lingering issues associated therewith.

The purpose of VOICE is to bridge differences and to provide comfort and support to boys of African descent. The members of VOICE can be assured that their cultural needs will be met and they will be free to express themselves while fostering brotherhood.

I once heard Gloria Ladson-Billings, the modern-day educational leader who coined the expression *culturally relevant pedagogy*,[113] which shifted the paradigm for my generation of teachers and whose writings helped me reexamine student achievement gaps as preparation gaps, describe Anna Julia Cooper as one with a plan for our race. This was a relay of memory, for I am nothing if not a student of Black women educators. I see the connectivity from my mother to my graduate school advisor and the dozens of Black women educators who poured into me. In a time and space far removed from what Dr. Cooper experienced, I found a kindredness in her words. She extended her remarks in *A Voice from the South* to say, "Only the BLACK WOMAN can say 'when and where I enter, in the quiet, undisputed dignity of my womanhood, without violence and without suing or special patronage, then and there the whole Negro race enters with me.' Is it not evident then that as individual workers for this race we must address ourselves with no half-hearted zeal to this feature of our mission? The need is felt and must be recognized by all."

Lavette Coney entered The Fessenden School and certainly made room for the entire race to enter. This is why I find it all the more divine that my journey to tell this story, which began with a chance reading of James Anderson's book, *The Education of Blacks in the South 1860–1935*, occurred only after Coney's unceremonious departure from the school. For me, it is a duty to ensure VOICE takes pride in her legacy, pays homage, and pays it forward.

Since 2022, VOICE stoles have been awarded to graduating ninth graders and departing eighth graders as they fulfill the rite of passage at Fessenden.

CHAPTER 5

Voice is equally beloved at Fessenden Academy. The Student Voice was a school newsletter circulated during the tenure of John A. Buggs. This cover depicts how Fessenden students understood their lives. Source: Fessenden Academy archives maintained by Amistad Research Center,
New Orleans, LA.

T he National Association of Independent Schools (NAIS) People of Color Conference (PoCC) and the Center for Black Teacher Development's Black Men in Education Convening (BMEC) are the educational conferences I attend most often. Understanding these gatherings and why I am among a relatively small handful with a foothold in both spaces offers tremendous insight into our story. The stakes are exceptionally high for this generation of Black students, their families, and the Black educators they desperately need. These conferences and their origins also frame the transition of the historical Fessenden Academy to today's proud Fessenden Elementary School.

The NAIS website states: "In 1986, NAIS hosted the first National Conference for Teachers and Administrators of Color in Independent Schools in Reston, Virginia. Two hundred people from 25 states attended the first conference, which later became the NAIS People of Color Conference (PoCC). This conference grew out of early equity initiatives at NAIS and was intended to be a place where faculty and staff of color, whose numbers represented a small portion of the workforce in independent schools, could come together to talk about their experiences, find support, and make progress in their career advancement." I have been fortunate to meet educators who are connected to the original two hundred, and each of my predecessors at Exeter and Fessenden attended at least one of the thirty-seven conferences to date. In 1993, the program grew to serve independent school students with the Student Diversity Leadership Conference (SDLC).

PoCC began as an affinity space, and the effort to ensure students similarly found respite, guidance, and affirmation away from their home campuses was an exercise of duty. However, and most notably, people of color does not mean exclusively Black. From the beginning, there was an acknowledgment that people of color, or otherwise non-white educators, shoulder a burden and take up a fight in their schools as well. While Black educators and their students are the blueprint and represent the largest demographic, meeting as a Black affinity group was only part of the program. Today, PoCC and SDLC boast an unparalleled national reach, serving roughly eight thousand attendees each year. Endowed funds or relatively large operating budgets at over two thousand NAIS member schools go a long way to cover the expense of sending cohorts each year. Former students have described the SDLC program as a life-changing experience, and PoCC has become a sort of family reunion for me. Within the last decade, PoCC and SDLC have emerged as diversity, equity, and inclusion conferences addressing a wide range of topics with the goal of improving independent schools, if not in practice, then certainly in how people of color feel about them.

As a new independent school teacher, I was uninterested in anything labeled for people of color. For me, it sounded too much like colored people, and without fully understanding the origins or methods, I was convinced that the PoCC had little to offer me. At the time, I saw myself as a Black mathematician turned high school teacher, and I wanted to develop my professional craft in that particular order. Math came first, and I took pride in that, but I was also unapologetically Black, Muslim, Philadelphian, and a public school graduate. None of these identities seemed explicitly pronounced at the conference. I also had a working knowledge of how diversity and the rhetoric of people of color did little to improve the material conditions of Black people. Despite carrying the heaviest stigma, much like affirmative action, Black folks were seldom the primary beneficiaries of these efforts.

It took some time, but eventually I came to see that standing in contrast to the lily-white aesthetic of a New England boarding school and the politics of privilege, blackness alone could not serve as an organizing tool, nor would it remedy my loneliness. Students would often escape to my classroom or office, but finding a single Black colleague to sit next to was not a luxury I enjoyed most days. I sought the company of those I did not need to explain myself to, or for whom I was not so obviously a token of their non-racism or a window into the Black culture. I cherished relationships with colleagues with whom I shared years of tenure, academic discipline, and worldview, but being a person of color in that environment was a unique experience. I began to build community with the same people of color I initially shielded. It said more about the generally unwelcoming nature of our place of work and the apathy shown by our nearest neighbors than it did about our individual racial politics. This is when the purpose of PoCC became clear to me.

Elsewhere, students living at or below the poverty line are typically assigned to the most budget-strapped public schools. Born out of the challenging conditions presented to Black men in and around the Philadelphia public school system, BMEC was founded in 2014 when roughly a dozen Black male educators came together at a local high school to strategize and make fellowship. Often spread out across different schools, there was no formal network to help develop, recruit, or retain Black men in the classroom. We could be found monitoring the hallways, coaching on the playing field, and perhaps within the administration. Still, we were absent from the most consequential position for students who resembled us. The reasons were not unique to Philadelphia or public schools per se. They were, in fact, historic in nature, undoubtedly structural by design, yet also exacting on the individual. My mentor, Sharif El-Mekki, was the principal of Mastery Charter, Shoemaker Campus at the time. As a veteran educator, inspiring organizer, and school leader, he was chosen to be the founder of this upstart movement. However, El-Mekki would be the first to remind me that teaching a Black child is a revolutionary act, and Black teachers have been political since the beginning. A once proud and noteworthy profession has seen a steady decline in representation. I still recall the staggering two-percent statistic from my first time attending BMEC: Black men account for just two percent of teachers in the United States.

In 2008, I thought I was following the natural course. After student-teaching in Philadelphia, I graduated from Cheyney University with a degree in mathematics and secondary education. I soon followed my brother and sister-in-law to Delaware State University to pursue a terminal degree in applied mathematics. In addition to graduate school, I continued my work as a residential counselor at Devereux's Pennsylvania campus, serving students with mental and behavioral health challenges. Tasked with the daily supervision of adjudicated minors during their school day and their transition to the residential program, I wanted to be their classroom teacher more than I cared to be a disciplinarian. So, five years later, when I sought stable employment at a Delaware alternative school to help support my young family through the graduate school years, the school that hired me to teach math also got an educator highly qualified to work with the most demanding student profiles.

The hardest part of the job was not the students, their behavior, or teaching them despite any existing prerequisite gaps, but the school system. In a nutshell, I defied conventional expectations. I could grasp abstract mathematical concepts, lecture about them at the university, and make them accessible to high school students diagnosed with dyscalculia or having math anxiety, while making it look cool. This made me a threat in many ways. I was young, Black, and gifted. Additionally, if the state standards required students to know the difference between an incenter, a centroid, and a circumcenter, I could teach it. I would also debate with colleagues and district-level curriculum specialists about the utility of those concepts and the mandated pacing guidelines. If a student were to ask, *When are we ever going to use this in real life,* I could reply, *Well, never, unless you want to become a math teacher like me, or spin a basketball on your finger, or study interior design, or become an engineer.* The discussion that ensued allowed me to explain that there are skills, math being one of the foremost, which serve as a gatekeeper. Mastering these skills gives you the key, and for all that math could illuminate for you, the real question is: what do you want to do with your very *real* life?

The problem I encountered was that teachers and students were not supposed to question school policy. More precisely, decisions were made for us, and while we were entitled to our opinions, expertise was reserved for those with the least proximity to the classroom. I was expected to teach critical thinking skills but not apply critical analysis to what was taught. That said, the more significant problem was deciding on any given day how to align classroom management, discipline, rapport, and my sense of justice within an unjust landscape. Ironically, I began to earn disfavor for being the teacher who could relate particularly well to those Black boys that other teachers struggled to manage.

I never asked students to skip class or ignore the rules. I did not ask them to stay after the bell to kick it. Quite the opposite, I pressed for my students to hurry on to their next class. But still, I was made to feel as if I was harboring escapees. Eventually, formal write-ups were followed by class visits, and suddenly, I was on the administration's radar. Colleagues began complaining about me as much as they did about some of my favorite students. I am sure I seemed like a defense attorney when it came to behavior. I could not excuse the actions of many of my students, but I understood their missteps as circumstantial and not a reflection of their character, upbringing, or what we should expect of them. Nonetheless, our school rules mirrored the state's criminal code. I was caught between a desire to save students and the need for safety, at times, from those same students.

In *Fugitive Pedagogy: Carter G. Woodson and the Art of Black Teaching,* Jarvis Givens writes, "Black education was a fugitive project from its inception—outlawed and defined as a criminal act regarding the slave population in the southern states and, at times, too, an object of suspicion and violent resistance in the North." This parallel between illegality on the one hand and the pursuit of knowledge on the other is foundational to school pride and racial pride. In his first chapter, Givens cites the enslaver of Frederick Douglass, who said that a slave who learns to read and write against the will of his master was tantamount to "running away with himself." Today, in 2025, obstacles to learning continue. Public school teachers face legal restrictions in more than sixteen states for teaching race and racism in the classroom. These words I write are likely to be banned from a Florida classroom and romanticized with little consequence by an independent school reading group. There is no doubt that Black history is the target; pride and memory are at a crossroads with shame and power. This is the greatest miseducation.

****

In 1868, before there was a Fessenden Academy, Black Civil War veterans enjoyed a special tribute in the name of Union School. Ferdinand Stone Fessenden understood this and would not have recognized a school bearing his name. He believed in the vision of the Union School, and he confirmed this honor in his final will, deeding the land and buildings to the American Missionary Association (AMA) with the explicit intention that generations of Black children would come there to study. The people of Marion County had a partner in the national organization. By the mid-1910s, Fessenden Academy was the pride of the local community and the AMA home office in New York. Together, they sought to address a specific form of racism in Central Florida, utilizing resources both locally and globally. There would be disagreements between Black folks on the ground in Florida and some within the leadership structure of the AMA. Still, the key dilemma endured: in the face of overt racism and subversive attacks, what is the function of education for the sons and daughters of freedpersons, and how can we make it accessible?

An 1893 *American Missionary* column posed this same question with the headline, "How Much Shall the Negro be Educated?" It instructs, "There are three answers to this in the South. The first is that he should not be educated at all, for it will lift him above his station. The second is, that he should have education enough to make him a better servant, laborer, or mechanic. The third, held by the few more liberal-minded Southern people, is that he should be educated as a white man is, for he is a man and must be prepared for all his duties to his country, the world and to God."[114] The North was no better in its application of educational access for Black people, but the religious paternalism inherent in this missionary fervor had a tremendous staying power. Simultaneously, Southern segregation was justified as the will of God. Neither pursuit was holy but rather political and controlling. Nothing evinced this tension more than the struggle over what Black students would study for the next one hundred years: vocational arts or liberal arts.

The most influential Black educator of the time, Booker T. Washington, was a leading proponent of vocational training. Some of his supporters desired Black labor for racially exploitative ends, while others saw the matter as more practical. Washington's industrial and agricultural arts-driven Tuskegee Institute in Alabama rivaled many AMA-supported, liberal arts-focused colleges, such as Fisk University in Tennessee. Both colleges originated as Normal Schools with strong teacher preparation programs before expanding their offerings. By the 1910s, the debate over curriculum had shaped not only Black colleges but also secondary and common schools.

Like many rural or remote locations, the areas surrounding Fessenden Academy had a desire for labor and strict racial norms, also known as Black Codes, which, for example, made it illegal for any *able-bodied* Black adult to be seen sitting idle.[115] In the decades following the Civil War, parents began seeking better futures for their children. Pursuing formal education offered options away from the sharecropping economy, and most poignantly, literacy was a mark of pride. Early on, schoolhouses were the epicenter of hope, with children occupying the seats during the day and adults at night. Education allowed workers to negotiate less exploitative contracts, retain wealth, start businesses, and file legal claims. Yet, this dream of a better life with previously closed doors now slightly ajar relied heavily on access. Pride in this progress, racially and personally, would soon encourage a class-based hierarchy of life outcomes, professional trade, and value to the race. Pride was and is an entendre, and without an appreciation for how education frames this viewpoint, pride can be divisive. Washington's 1895 *Atlanta Compromise Speech* perhaps captured this best: "No race can prosper till it learns that there is as much dignity in tilling the fields as in writing a poem."[116]

Joseph Wiley, a graduate of Fisk University, was neither a direct critic nor disciple of Washington, but he was responsible for answering the curricular question for Fessenden. He advanced the school's mission to demonstrate that education was a tool for moral improvement and racial uplift despite the odds against him and the student body. In doing so, Wiley came to embody what an investment in a liberal education could look like for a generation still economically dependent on field labor. At the same time, Fessenden was not free of cost. The price, albeit modest for the time, still required a tremendous sacrifice from families and was cost-prohibitive for others. Private schools were and remain an entendre. For Fessenden, this meant the highest quality of instruction for a limited number of students, but it also guaranteed autonomy for their teachers. Nevertheless, far too many Black children needed a place to learn, and given the scale of injustice, privatization could never serve the greater good. This fundamental contradiction within the school's missionary vision would eventually come to a head.

Independent schools and private schools are often used interchangeably, and the technicalities are usually a matter of the school's governance and design. However, under Wiley's care, as was the case for many Black schools at this time, Fessenden's role within the community challenges even these assumptions. Left to the discretion of the state, Black students in Marion County would have gone ignored for decades. The county's first Black school, Howard Academy, was named after a former enslaver who donated the land, but the Freedman's Bureau was responsible for the school's founding in 1866. Established in the War Department by an 1865 act of Congress, the Freedmen's Bureau was responsible for all matters involving refugees, freedmen, and abandoned lands following the end of the Civil War. "The Bureau generally supplied buildings for schools, transportation for teachers, and relied on aid societies and freedmen to pay for teacher salaries."[117] Both Fessenden and Howard faced local and state discrimination, and their independence resulted from that. School fees did not make them private; quite the opposite. In 1866, Florida's first and only tax to fund schools fell exclusively on Black men with prejudice.[118] Essentially, there was no remorse or reparation for centuries of criminalizing Black education under the threat of death. So, if Black schools were to exist, then white Floridians wanted no part.

Economics are often a proxy for emotion, hate being foremost. The state's underfunding of schools reflected a hostility held by the larger white population. Notions of supremacy and inferiority often sparked cognitive dissonance at the sight of Black progress, and to reclaim authority, every tool

171

was weaponized. Black bodies remained a commodity, and Black schools posed a threat to the labor market. Still, beyond this, the influence of Northerners on the affairs of a former Confederate state was met with swift and strong resistance. In particular, attempts to sabotage and undercut the work of the Freedmen's Bureau made it short-lived and left it incomplete. Florida's Freedman's Bureau office closed in 1870, after providing some relief in its attempts for justice. The late historian and Professor Emeritus Joe M. Richardson wrote of the Bureau, "It created a small independent land-owning class of freedmen and guided them politically, but it could not induce the white South to accept its former slaves as equal."[119] The Bureau successfully established the public school system for both races, and with the federal government removed, Howard Academy came under the purview of Marion County and was subjected to the effects of segregation. Where politicians failed, northern philanthropy and Black self-determination took over. Fessenden remained independent with the AMA's support, but mainly because the community understood the value proposition.

Joseph Wiley's leadership ensured the school would prosper for years to come. The mutual dependency between Fessenden and its Black neighbors required attention, as did the precarious situation with white folk, and Wiley was an effective diplomat and educator. In 1901, he delivered a speech to Black farmers urging them to stay on their land. He gave regular speeches at churches and farm conventions and supported the work of public schools. Fessenden housed an industrial arts program that provided skill development, and when opportunities for campus projects arose, Wiley employed local Black artisans. Politically, Wiley supported the Temperance movement and urged moral uprightness at school. Patriotism and being a law-abiding citizen were important daily lessons at Fessenden. When a former Fessenden student was murdered in 1909, it is reported, "Wiley was summoned to join the posse," and counseled caution in the face of righteous anger.[120] These actions earned him significant favor with the white population of Marion County, and when the Black vote was stripped away, Wiley was one of a handful of land-owning, educated Black men left on the ballot.

Mastering this balance between constituencies was critical to keeping Fessenden safe and supported. Rather than closing the institution off to outsiders, Wiley invited white officials onto campus to display the range of courses and his politely talented students. As a Fisk graduate, Wiley appreciated liberal education, but he was savvy enough to present the skills of industry in a way that was disarming to white sensibilities. His charm and initiative earned Fessenden funding from staunch segregationalists in both the county and state superintendent offices. He understood that Fessenden needed to serve its time and location.

Fessenden students received training to be gardeners, textile workers, and carpenters, not only for future occupations, but also in service to the school they loved. This fiscally sustainable approach encouraged entrepreneurship and skilled hands overall, which inspired independence rather than dependence on a racial caste society designed for exploitation. Within the lifespan of a freedperson, Black wealth grew. Fessenden relied on this middle class in Marion County and beyond for prospective students and support. When Booker T. Washington toured Florida in 1912, he stopped in Ocala to speak to a large crowd of Black and white residents. He also visited and spoke to students at Fessenden. As a sign of local progress following Washington's visit, the Florida

Negro Business League opened a savings bank in 1913 with customers of both races.[121] Fessenden's Joseph Wiley served as the bank's first vice president.

Along with much praise, Wiley also earned some detractors. Namely, his demands on faculty resulted in grievances filed against him. While he was known as kind and caring toward students, teachers saw him as harsh. The most distant of all the AMA's schools, Wiley held a lot of discretionary power. The subsequent burden of independence required Wiley to press for the highest standards from his teachers while navigating biases from AMA officials. Seen as having too much self-determination, Wiley was asked to resign by AMA Superintendent Paul H. Douglass in 1913. Thoroughly immersed in his calling and passion for Fessenden, Wiley declined the request. His implementation of a functional education—combining both liberal and vocational disciplines—was best suited for this environment and is central to understanding his legacy.[122]

May 1915 would be the last time Principal Wiley's words would appear in print for Congregational Church members and readers of their national publication, *The American Missionary*. He wrote, "The basic idea of a mission school supported by the church must be personal Christianity. Geometrical propositions, chemistry tables, dead languages, athletics incorporated in the school life, are almost futile if the students of these schools are not trained in Christian character."[123] Wiley did more than preach. Fessenden students were introduced to banking, building construction, community service, and the Bible.

Known by many as the Tuskegee of Florida, Fessenden established an alumni body that expanded to more than one thousand graduates under Principal Wiley, and the value of Fessenden's physical plant increased by four hundred percent. To appreciate the extent of this accomplishment, the Fessenden Academy Wiley built in 1915, would appraise for hundreds of millions of dollars in 2025, after accounting for inflation. And the descendants of his students could number in the hundreds of thousands. Additionally, the pipeline of Black teachers that sprang forth from Wiley's tutelage brought his spirit to an uncountable number of learners throughout the state. Acknowledgement of his work came from all corners, even from would-be enemies. This made his inexplicable disappearance all the more devastating, draping a deep sorrow over the school. The close-knit Fessenden community included his grieving wife, loyal community members, and students as young as eight years old who would have lost a hero.

It is difficult to conclude how many Black people went missing during the first quarter of the twentieth century, but Florida was nonetheless notorious for the killing of Black men. A recent Equal Justice Initiative report lists the nation's twenty-five most hazardous areas in regard to lynching between 1877 and 1950. Florida appears four times: Orange, Columbia, Polk, and Marion counties.[124] Inappropriateness with, or harm to white women, voting, political organizing, theft of property, or assault of a white man were all leading excuses. Large-scale violence and mass killings, like the 1920 Ocoee and 1923 Rosewood massacres, claimed lives, displaced entire Black populations, and, in the cases of Ocoee and Rosewood, occurred only a day's journey from the Fessenden campus. The brutality is hard to capture in words, and yet the aftermath reverberates across

175

generations and sits with us today. When cries for justice fall on deaf ears, unspeakable crimes painfully fade into silence.

According to researcher and sociologist Stewart E. Tonlay, between 1882 and 1930, Florida had the highest per capita rate of lynching.[125] Author Margaret Vandiver discusses the region around Fessenden in her analysis of lynching and legal executions throughout the entire South. By 1930, a total of nineteen Black men were lynched in Marion County. Hundreds of white men, women, and children witnessed the public gore, yet perpetrators were never prosecuted. Klan activity was vibrant throughout the county for decades. While some white residents found the lawlessness distasteful, large mobs would often overrun law enforcement to seize Black captives with impunity.[126] It was no secret that this brutality was intentional, yet any citizen, regardless of race, risked their lives and livelihood by speaking out.

For a generation born during the height of such repression, murder was the likely explanation for Wiley's disappearance. A National Association for the Advancement of Colored People (NAACP) field agent confirmed this suspicion while investigating a missing person in 1937. "Ocala did something of this kind…years ago with one Prof. Wiley, a respectable school teacher."[127] During this time, Black people had no guarantees of due process, and illegal vigilante justice was not out of the question for any Black person alleged to have broken the law. Far worse, a violation of the social order, such as resisting personal degradation, not paying deference to a white man, or advances towards a white woman, perceived, fabricated, or otherwise, could result in the spectacle of lynching. These extrajudicial killings were undeniably acts of racial terrorism. In cases where families were able to collect and bury their dismembered, sexually mutilated, or even burned loved ones' bodies, they received no justice nor sympathy from the state. However, for the missing and feared dead, the lack of closure was its own form of torture. They had no case to plead, so, as with Wiley, questions persist today. The only certainty we have is to acknowledge that the truth has been long buried.

The apparatus of *hear no evil, see no evil*, was instrumental in imposing racial dominance. Beyond the personal coping method of shutting down to deal with the obvious trauma, children were taught at an early age to remain hushed about certain things — to not ask questions whose answers were too painful to speak, to allow the ancestors' anguish to rest with them. With no justice or protection, generations of Black survivors learned to defend themselves at all costs, to keep things within, and to trust no one. And for good reason: at its peak, Klan membership in Florida climbed to more than sixty thousand dues-paying members.[128] In *The Invisible Empire: The Ku Klux Klan in Florida,* Michael Newton compiles graphic evidence that demonstrates how collusion between the law, business, and nondescript white residents worked to advance a code. "Since 1868, the KKK has been a force to reckon with in Florida...Klansmen have marched, elected civic leaders, infiltrated law enforcement, and committed crimes." Lurking beneath the many testimonies of episodic horror, the political arm of oppression rallied most ferociously against Black suffrage and the desegregation of schools.

By 1916, undeterred by a palpably treacherous atmosphere, Fessenden Academy took steps to move forward, and the AMA appointed Rev. H. S. Barnwell as Principal. *The American Missionary* remained silent about the circumstances that necessitated new leadership. For their uninformed readers, a

Wiley-to-Barnwell transition would not seem out of the ordinary, and from the periodic updates on the school, few would guess any setbacks had occurred. Locally, enrollment held steady, and Fessenden remained one of the most attractive options for prospective students. Glowing reports like those written by AMA Rev. George W. Moore suggest that by 1917, Fessenden was indeed an oasis from the threat of harm:

Having just come from the land of snow and ice I could scarcely believe my eyes when I found myself in this land of sunshine, flowers, and oranges. A number of barefoot boys and girls on their way to school give picturesqueness to the scene. The school has a post office with three mails daily from local trains, which stop daily on the signal, and the telephone brings the place in touch with the surrounding country. I find that the intellectual, industrial, and spiritual life of the school is receiving much emphasis. The religious life of the school is expressed through the Sunday school, preaching services, Christian Endeavor, and daily chapel exercises; while the community needs are reached through the Y.M.C.A and Y.W.C.A. and the services of teachers and the principal. A farmers' conference and association is organized in the community, with the Academy as the center of its meetings. While Fessenden has done a large and thoroughly good work in character building and in its contributions to good citizenship, a still larger opportunity awaits its future. The harmonious relationship of both races has made the work of cooperation for the good of the people especially fruitful.[129]

If racial harmony ever could exist under Jim Crow law, it required Black Americans to know and stay in their place. Ironically, a school campus that offered several dozen lush acres, loving staff, learning to stimulate the mind, and prayer to feed the soul did just that. However, as we will soon see, Fessenden would also become a place to organize against the forces that threatened Black prosperity.

Barnwell successfully managed the school for five years and later became the Executive Secretary of Church Mission for the American Missionary Association in the South. Succeeding Barnwell was New York-born William Kindle, and in 1922, the school's name was officially changed from Fessenden Academy and Industrial School to Fessenden Academy. Following Kindle's administration, John M. Moore, Aurelius S. Scott, Rev. Leonard F. Morse, and Ripley S. Sims would contribute as leaders throughout the late 1920s and early 1930s.

In addition to Fessenden's relative safety, the campus was especially well-resourced. Classroom teachers were of the highest caliber, and master craftspersons taught vocational skills. This was a far cry from conditions statewide, where segregation allowed for discrimination in school assignment, allotment of educational funds, length of the academic year, student per capita funding, and teacher pay.[130] In 1918, Florida invested $4,383,455 in white schools and a tenth of that, $443,600, in Black schools for a per capita breakdown of $41.37 per white child attending school daily and $10.93 per Black child.[131] By 1927, the funding gap widened to 31 million dollars and 1.7 million dollars, respectively. Racist policies were so deeply entrenched that even funds allocated for the most destitute, or specifically for Black schools, were rerouted in Florida. To survive, Black schools had to be self-funded or supported externally.

Established in 1867, the Peabody Fund, named after Massachusetts-born George Peabody, the cofounder of what later became J. P. Morgan & Co., supported Black schools at a fraction of its investment in white schools with comparable enrollment.[132] Much like the Freedman's Bureau, Peabody funds were used during Reconstruction to supplement the creation of a white public school system in Florida at the expense of Black or integrated schools. In 1914, one of the final disbursements of Peabody funds went to the Slater Fund, an endowment started by Rhode Island Congregational Church member John F. Slater with the explicit desire to assist the education of freedpersons.

The Rosenwald Fund, named after Julius Rosenwald, famously helped build thousands of Black schoolhouses throughout the South when the former Confederate States refused to support schools for Black youth equitably. In speaking of the Rosenwald Fund, Florida Superintendent William S. Cawthorn, in 1928, wrote, "Negroes themselves have contributed more money to financing these buildings than the Fund. The Negroes through their contributions become thoroughly imbued with the feeling that the buildings are theirs and theirs to maintain in first class conditions. It is hoped that the financial aid given toward construction of schoolhouses will influence officials to more adequately care for the needs of Negro children. With this hope in mind, aid has been granted at a decreasing scale.... It is hoped that school officials will realize their obligations to the Negro citizen and provide for them voluntarily without receiving large stimulative assistance from philanthropy." In this same annual report showing the degree to which Black public schools suffered under a separate and unequal system, Fessenden Academy is studied along with the state's Black institutions for higher learning, which later became Bethune Cookman University, Florida Memorial University,

Edward Waters University, and Florida Agricultural and Mechanical University.[133]

By anyone's standard, Fessenden was elite and prestigious, certainly among Florida's secondary schools, regardless of race. State officials were content with its one privately funded Black school. Still, the diplomacy of the AMA included the painful practice of turning many of its schools over to local authorities. The AMA's mission was not to create an exclusive learning experience. They sought to remedy the criminalization of Black education and offer a buffer from Southern racism. In this way, the AMA aligned with the mission of Black Americans who believed schools should be multipurpose institutions serving the local community. Initiatives like adult education, economic cooperatives, teacher development, and college preparation were uniquely Black school services during this era. Naively, the AMA's hope that Black schools could thrive in the hands of Jim Crow rested upon the unrealistic dream of *improved race relations* – that somehow separate-and-unequal would become separate-and-just.

Fred Brownlee, the AMA's longest-serving secretary, made several visits to Fessenden during his tenure and was impressed each time. "Brownlee joined the AMA with limited experience with African Americans, but eventually became the least paternalistic and most aggressive advocate of equal rights of any AMA secretary."[134] In 1925, Secretary Brownlee described an encounter with a Florida businessman on his way to Fessenden:

He proceeded to tell me how much he knew about the Negro than I did; how educating the 'nigger' was unfitting him of his place; what he would do personally if a 'nigger' ever aspired to vote or to become part of the legislature, and particularly what he would do if colored policeman ever tried to arrest him. All of this was familiar to me, but what I said to him was flatly denied as the truth. He did not care to hear it, as a matter of fact. It made him nervous to hear about educated and refined Negroes.[135]

During Brownlee's career with the AMA, he served as an advisor to many schools and universities. Earning honorary doctor's degrees from Howard University, Tougaloo College, Oberlin College, and Ohio State University, Brownlee communed with educational leaders across the country. He served as trustee to Talledaga College, Dillard University, Tillotson College, and LeMoyne College. In particular, Brownlee's role with AMA and his position on Fisk University's board of trustees brought him into correspondence with the renowned public intellectual and world historian, W. E. B. Du Bois. They exchanged many letters, including an offer to advertise AMA schools in the national magazine founded by Du Bois during his time with the NAACP.[136] As an active supporter of Du Bois's contributions to fighting the race problem, Brownlee was likely present or at least aware of the 1924 graduation speech Du Bois delivered at Fisk University, in which he identified, "Two extreme attitudes which a Negro college might take with regard to the surrounding South; it might teach that the case is hopeless; that no Negro can expect to be a man in this country with the present attitude and determination of the whites. Or it might go to the opposite extreme and say that all is well; that the best thought of the country is tending toward justice and that the Negro's only hindrance is himself. Neither of these positions is tenable…the fact that there are here forces of advancement and uplift, that there are forces of evil and

182

retrogression, and that it is for the educated man to find a way amid these difficulties." In a 1930 speech at Howard University, Du Bois remarked, "the object of education was not to make men carpenters, but make carpenters men."[137]

As we have seen, Fessenden Academy confronted many of the same issues facing Black colleges and universities. In 1937, the school's curriculum, finances, and safety all fell under the leadership of Fisk graduate Josie B. Sellers. Despite having no secondary school teaching experience, Secretary Brownlee was convinced that Sellers had the vision and skill to make Fessenden a community school. And his instincts were proven right. As a certified social worker and college professor, Principal Sellers had the brilliance and personality to carry Fessenden forward. During her tenure, a demonstration farm was established, allowing students to work collaboratively with community members. The senior math class opened and sold student shares in their own Fessenden Fund and Trust Company. Additionally, Sellers introduced a student advisory council and a school newspaper.[138] Triumphs like these and reports of how Fessenden students, under the tutelage of instructor Wesley E. Walthall, travelled to Cotton Valley School in Alabama and built a six-bedroom, two-bath, cozy teacher's cottage, are perhaps why Fessenden has the distinction of being the last of nearly five hundred AMA schools.

Secretary Brownlee hired Ruth Morton in 1935 to be the AMA's Director of Community Schools, but their combined will did not turn Fessenden into this epicenter of living and learning. Brownlee and Morton worked behind the scenes to negotiate for time and independence from church officials who believed that local school boards should take over AMA schools sooner. Against Brownlee's objection, the AMA legally ceded control to the Board of Home Missions (BHM) of the Congregational Church.[139] The BHM and AMA shared a philosophy for community schools, but the move would prove significant for the remaining AMA institutions because the new leadership considered their role as a non-government entity to be temporary and complete. Nonetheless, Fessenden Academy became noteworthy then and remains hallowed ground today, as an example of Black adults establishing a village for their children. Fessenden students continued to have access to apprenticeships and scholarships, and by the mid-1940s, of the remaining AMA secondary schools, Fessenden sent the highest proportion of graduates to college. In 1942, Principal Sellers passed the mantle of leadership on to a 27-year-old Dillard and Fisk graduate, John A. Buggs, who undertook the final relay of Fessenden's independence.

Principal Buggs ensured that Fessenden students were introduced to ecology, economics, geography, history, political science, rural sociology, and statistics, alongside community living, health, leisure, and work. The *Negro problem* was not avoided. Students explored the issues facing minority groups and experienced real-world solutions found through cooperatives, credit unions, farm organizations, labor unions, and vocational guidance. What Buggs called an *experiment in education*, Brownlee called the most advanced understanding of a functional education he had yet encountered and, in 1949, praised Buggs as "the best man I have ever met in the field of secondary education and school administration." Constantly seeking to improve, Buggs encouraged the faculty to revise their offerings and build a curriculum tailored to each student's path to college, trade school, or occupation. The school also demonstrated tremendous dexterity in utilizing its three-hundred-acre campus, which provided experiential learning opportunities for multiple crafts. Academics had a clear purpose and direction, encompassing citizenship, Christian ethics, home life, self-expression, vocation, and wellness. Extracurricular activities included drama, journalism, music, a radio station, and student government, but Buggs's tenure is best known for his community outreach and political organizing. [140]

Richardson writes, "Buggs's greatest community service was in advocating civil rights, encouraging political action, and training veterans. Even before the war ended, Buggs conceived the idea of helping veterans complete high school or gain technical job skills." The opportunity at Fessenden defined true service to servicemen. For the greater part of a century, Jim Crow laws limited opportunities in education and employment. Initially, the armed forces offered hope, but the experience of war proved far from equal. Returning home, racial discrimination, indeed in the South, continued in the denial of federal benefits set aside for soldiers. Countless studies have confirmed the government's failure to support Black veterans. A claim headlined in the 1946 *Pittsburgh Courier*, at the time the largest Black newspaper, described the situation, "as though the GI Bill had been earmarked for *White Veterans Only*."[141] Even more desponding, Black Floridians returned to a racial prejudice so deep that Nazi prisoners of war incarcerated in about a dozen Florida detention camps were treated with more respect than Black men in uniform.[142] The initiatives led by Buggs aimed to address a genuine American crisis. With the assistance of the AMA and a postwar emergency program, a $100,000 technical training art building was built on campus. Fessenden was then able to offer courses in auto mechanics, business, carpentry, commercial dietetics, furniture building, radio servicing, tailoring, and typing to nearly eighty veterans.[143]

At Fessenden, the joint tenure of Sellers and Buggs spans the years of the Great Depression and World War II. These were extremely difficult times for AMA schools, which depended upon philanthropy and tuition dollars. Most schools did not survive, but the plan to sell off AMA schools for the greater good of public education dates back to before the Civil War. The AMA gave or sold property to local boards to expedite public access. Schools in Maryland, Kentucky, Tennessee, Georgia, and Louisiana were transferred to local control before 1880. And for the next fifty years, there was a steady process of downsizing the number of AMA schools while those on the ground reinvested to maintain quality, shift curriculum, defend *negro education*, care for the community, and fight against racism. "Brownlee in 1929 described the AMA's policy as 'progressive absorption' and 'cooperation'—that is, the AMA would transfer schools to local authorities when there was a duplication."[144] And, where there were no suitable public schools for Black children to attend, the AMA would help local residents mount a legal claim backed by political action to force segregationists to respond to the needs of Black citizens.

Brownlee writes, "In the days when public schools in the South were 'inching along' the Association's schools were preparing hundreds of teachers."[145] In addition to supplying the skilled teacher workforce, AMA agents also became state and county officials, such as C. Thurston Chase, Florida's first superintendent of public instruction. Segregation was the law, and this meant unequal treatment under the law. The spiritual bankruptcy that denies children access to a classroom reveals a racism that defies human logic and decency. Individual AMA officials, no matter how progressive, liberal-minded, or rightly guided they believed they were, could not overturn a system. Unfortunately, it required something worldly.

The AMA's approach was different in every municipality, but the policy almost always required financially incentivizing states to adopt its current schools or open a new building for the Black students barred from the state's white public schools. In Georgia, a nearly one-hundred-year legacy of education dating back to the Civil War ended with the closure of Dorchester Academy in 1942. The factors were many, but the AMA's desire to see public schools free of tuition and supported by local government came in stages. White public schools existed for decades, but legal action threatening segregation eventually compelled reluctant county officials to build a separate Black public school. The AMA agreed to co-fund the project, understanding the risks and that true equality was unlikely. Brownlee and Morton met with Dorchester Academy families, asking permission to proceed with the plan by vote. They understood the greater good was having a public school open to everyone and acknowledged that initially, the new school would not meet the standards set by Dorchester Academy. Not a single negative vote was cast; yet the community's principled belief in public education and hope that the county and state would honor *separate and equal* schools eventually led to deep regret.[146]

Brownlee also described the process of closing an AMA school and turning it over to public school authorities as painful. In a 1950 memorandum, the year he resigned from the AMA, Brownlee wrote, "The parents looked askance at every step the

AMA took towards public schools. It was difficult for them to admit that each step was even in the right direction. From our end it was always easier to make decisions in New York than on the ground in conference with principals, parents, teachers and patrons."[147] Eric Anderson and Alfred A. Moses Jr. further quote from and write about Brownlee's statements in their 1999 book, *Dangerous Donations: Northern Philanthropy and Southern Black Education*: "The goal of public education seemed right, 'I took a long look, drew a long breathe,' and urged the AMA executive committee to go ahead with turning another school over to a white school board. And every time the Committee vote read like a death sentence to the people. To me the decision meant extended life, to the people it meant death. Invariably, it was impossible to carry the people with us in our conclusions." This tension clutches at the throat today. Serving the greater good meant prioritizing the majority of Black families who could not afford to pay tuition, and, without fail, enrollment increased each time an AMA school became public. Yet, hindsight allows us to ask whether negligence is better than delivering oneself into the hands of abusers.

During the mid-1930s, the economic situation intensified, and the AMA was forced to make more difficult decisions. In Greenwood, South Carolina, it took ten years of investment and deal-making to establish a public high school for Black students on the grounds of the Brewer Institute. The AMA paid salaries on a sliding scale and absorbed the cost of upkeep for the physical plant during the transition of control. The process concluded in 1935 when the AMA transferred all buildings and land to the local school board. The AMA set the condition for the state to maintain a free accredited high school, "and that the property be held in perpetuity for the welfare of African Americans." Similar steps were taken elsewhere; the AMA sold property for cents on the dollar and gave generous lease options to counties willing to partner. A sense of justice rarely inclined school boards. Instead, as in the case of Dorchester Academy, preserving Jim Crow required a separate public alternative rather than integration. And, as in the case of Brewer, the county became eligible for federal funding once they took ownership.[148]

Fessenden was one of a handful of exemptions during this era of downsizing and offloading. By 1927, the former Howard Academy offered relief by becoming the county's first Black public high school. And in 1933, Marion County signaled more change when they built a public elementary school adjacent to Fessenden Academy on two acres of land donated by the AMA. However, the new site was more of a satellite campus operating under Fessenden's direction. As the premier option for many families in the area, the community was not concerned about a potential closure of Fessenden. In fact, with Buggs's leadership, the community turned to Fessenden like never before. The veteran work program was closely tied to Buggs's philosophy, character, and politics. Beginning as an activist and helping to register the vote, Buggs was chosen to be the secretary of the Marion County NAACP in 1943, and Fessenden became a hub of political organizing. Richardson cites the Black-owned *Tampa Bulletin*'s estimate that Buggs added five thousand voters to Marion County's roll between 1944 and 1950. And Ruth Morton once remarked that Fessenden was the only place in Florida where Black politicians could strategize to get out the vote safely. Faculty and students all played a role in registration drives, and in

1949, with Buggs' encouragement, a NAACP youth council emerged on campus.

To emphasize the significance of such political activity, we must recall the times. In 1934, Harry T. and Harriette Moore founded Florida's Brevard County branch of the NAACP. The Moores were public school teachers who became politically active and famously fought for equal pay for teachers alongside the famed civil rights lawyer and future Supreme Court Justice Thurgood Marshall. When a 1944 ruling outlawed white-only primaries, Harry registered more than one hundred thousand Black voters for the Florida Democratic Party. As NAACP State Secretary for Florida, he also investigated lynchings and extrajudicial murder, and between 1949 and 1951 worked tirelessly to overturn the wrongful conviction of a group of young Black men for an alleged rape. The men were granted a new trial, but the local sheriff shot two of the defendants, killing one and critically injuring the other. Harry called for the sheriff's indictment and arrest. Six weeks later, on Christmas evening and the couple's 25th wedding anniversary, the KKK coordinated the first assassination of an NAACP official. After a night of celebrating, the Moores went to bed, and a bomb exploded under the floorboards of their bedroom. Because of segregation, Harry passed away while in transit to the nearest hospital that would treat him. Harrietta passed away nine days later.[149] Despite a massive federal investigation, several state inquiries, and a national outcry, including the galvanizing freedom song written by Langston Hughes, "A Ballad of Harry Moore" and despite international shame, in the form of William Patterson and Paul Robeson citing the Moore case in their *We Charge Genocide* petition presented to the United Nations General Assembly in 1951, no one was charged for the double murder.

That spring, Fessenden was on high alert as rumors churned that Buggs could be a target. The late reporter Paul Weeks, who covered and befriended Buggs during the Los Angeles Civil Rights struggle of the 1960s, wrote: "John's turn came around in the 1940s when the Fessenden Academy for Black youth in Florida named him as its director. And after hours, as an activist for the NAACP, he registered blacks to vote. Shortly, the organization's state secretary was assassinated, and they said John would be 'next.' John was scheduled to give the graduation address in 1951. Word spread that the professor had a gun of his own under the formal gown. His speech was punctuated by applause—not gunfire."

The 1951 graduation was the sunset for an era. It concluded an eighty-three-year legacy of Black independent education, sealing a remarkable tradition with a ritual of pride. The usual tears from saying goodbye to the senior class flowed alongside a stream of memories more fitting of a funeral. As Buggs's final performance as principal, it was not the end that he or the community desired. In 1949, following the closure of many peer schools, Buggs proposed keeping Fessenden alive by converting it into an interracial prep school, but that motion failed. That same year, Marion County's public Black high school began offering bus service to outlying areas, which ultimately signaled the closure of Fessenden Academy. In Buggs's final campaign to the state of Florida, he suggested, with community support, that Fessenden become a junior college. This, too, failed. The fight to retain Fessenden's independence ended with an executive committee vote. On June 25, 1951, a headline in the national journal of the Congregational Christian Churches read, "Mission Accomplished." It continued, "At the meeting of the Executive Committee of our Board of Home Missions on April 17-18, action was taken authorizing the termination of work at Fessenden Academy, Martin, Florida, at the conclusion of the current academic year. This decision was made with mingled reluctance and satisfaction."

I do not have the words to capture the weight of a school closure juxtaposed with newfound opportunity. For some of the Fessenden faithful, the Academy was, as the retired Secretary Brownlee described, "a house of freedom, a house of refuge, a house of counsel, a house of prayer. It was as if the bottom had fallen out of the universe."[150] For others, the house was now open and ready to welcome family members.

Fessenden Academy students date unknown. Source: Fessenden Academy archives maintained by Amistad Research Center, New Orleans, LA.

CONCLUSION

Anything complete should have a beginning and an end. This project has spanned three years of research, encompassing content from the 1600s to the present day. However, as it concludes, I need to clarify the starting point. Teaching is a challenging profession, and like most, I am unapologetic about having a restorative summer. For the past decade, or more, my professional growth has included some form of return to Africa during the summer months. I have visited schools in Ghana, toured Senegal, taught students in Somaliland, trained teachers in South Africa, and worked with educational leaders in Zanzibar, but I have traveled most frequently to Egypt. I believe that all Black Americans should have the opportunity to experience the continent. And it has primarily been my privilege as an independent school educator with access to professional development funding that affords me such opportunity. This was the case again in the summer of 2024 when The Fessenden School supported my journey to the beginning.

The Nile River Basin connects eleven African countries: Burundi, Democratic Republic of the Congo, Egypt, Eritrea, Ethiopia, Kenya, Rwanda, South Sudan, Sudan, Tanzania, and Uganda. Flowing south to north, the Nile delivers vital nutrients for plant, animal, and human life, from the internal regions of Africa to the northernmost areas of Egypt. Thousands of years ago, the inhabitants of the land had a name for the rich soil surrounding the river. They called it Kemet, and in the ancient Medu Netchur language, known to the Greeks as hieroglyph, the world's oldest known writing system, Kemet translates to *black soil*. Kemet, or Black Land, is also the name given to the entire region we call Ancient Egypt, whose many empires began to form more than 5,000 years ago. Before my trip in 2024, I had a decent understanding of some of the great kingdoms, the massive treasures, the architecture, the pyramids, the shared religious traditions, and, of course, the controversy of race.

One of the biggest conspiracies in modern history has been to divorce Greek and Roman contributions from their Egyptian teachers, and to obscure the undeniable Blackness of Ancient Egypt's enduring legacy. Taken together, the basis for intellectual supremacy, religious hierarchy, and pride begins here. Years ago, I recall a faculty debate at a leading independent school about the course descriptions for classical languages. Colloquially known as Classics, the teaching of Latin and Greek is foundational for not only the most selective secondary schools but also for universities throughout the Western Hemisphere. Spoken by medieval Christians, if the everyday use of Latin died with the fall of the Roman Empire nearly 1,500 years ago, it was preserved as the word of choice for scholars, diplomats, and clergy. With the advent of European expansion and cross-continental imperialism, which began only 500 years ago, language fluency implied status, and this required a command of Latin and its derivatives. As the Portuguese, Spanish, French, English, and others came to the Americas, so too did Latin. The challenge has never been about teaching classical languages in school. It is about who and what we consider to be classical. There is no way to take race and religion out of this assessment. And, unfortunately, when schools allow rhetoric that suggests that the

Greeks and Romans were the *first to consider the human condition*, a sin has been committed.

In that faculty debate and far too many other discussions of similar merit, I tend to refer to the mathematicians of Alexandria. Names like Pythagoras and Euclid are well-known to students and teachers worldwide due to their significant contributions to the field of mathematics. Pythagoras, best known for the right-triangle theorem named in his honor, predates Euclid, who famously compiled the work of multiple thinkers into the *Elements of Geometry*, written nearly 2,300 years ago. This work, regarded by many Europeans as the most influential text in human history, other than the Bible, is considered a cornerstone of Western mathematics. But neither man was an autodidact; they were both Greeks who lived in Africa. They were teachers, and they were also students. At this point in the conversation, I usually clarify that the concept of race as we understand it did not exist during the time of the Ancient Egyptians. However, we are confident that the mathematicians who built the Great Pyramid, the astrologers whose science and spirituality was copied and pasted into Zodiac, the rulers whose riches sit in museums around the world, the artisans and the priests who dedicated their lives to constructing obelisks that reach the sky and tombs buried far below the sand, and those who died without mention had hair, skin color, and physical features that resemble people of African origin. Indeed, Alexandria is in Egypt, and Egyptians are Africans. Still, for me to suggest that the pinnacle of white civilization borrowed from a people we would call Black was blasphemous.

The hard truth is that race does not exist, but the effects of racism are very real. Today, most experts agree that race is a modern-day social construct, but many in society still assume that race has a scientific backing. The once firmly held belief in a racial hierarchy, or that a person's race was observable by the naked eye, detectable at the genetic level, and conferred specific traits, namely intelligence for reason, abstract thought, and design, has been disproven. These ideas, advanced through pseudoscience and taught in schools for centuries, have had a corrosive effect on our understanding of the world. In the field of Egyptology, the debate over the race of the Ancients dates back to the first European and American researchers who claimed discovery. They brought backward ideas about race to a people who were forward-thinking beyond our imagination.

In the summer of 2024, when I returned to the Nile Valley, I joined more than sixty other Black travelers from around the world who had signed up for The Kemet Study Tour. Leading the group were two professors from Howard University: Dr. Greg Carr, a law professor and Chair of the Department of Afro-American Studies, and Dr. Mario Beatty, President of The Association for the Study of Classical African Civilizations and a leading expert in Medu Netchur. The two-week program, offered through Knarrative, a membership-based online platform for Africana Studies founded by journalist and educator Karen Hunter, provided guided tours to ninety-five percent of Egypt's historical sites. We began where most travelers do in Cairo, with one of the seven wonders of the ancient world, the Giza plateau. We also toured the Egyptian Museum of Cairo and the newly opened Grand Egyptian Museum before heading south to Luxor and finally to Aswan. Most tourists do not leave Cairo, and most tour guides are not Nubian, the darker-toned Egyptians who trace their lineage to southern Egypt and northern Sudan, and whose people share a greater genetic similarity with the Ancients than any other ethnic group. It was in Luxor and Aswan, where I saw the temple and the tomb of Seti I, and any confusion about color vanished.

The timeline for Ancient Egypt begins approximately 7000 years ago with the Pre-Dynastic Period, followed by the emergence of the first pharaohs around 2000 years later. It concludes after the 30th Dynasty with Alexander the Great's conquest, three hundred years of Greco-Roman rule, and the last of the pharaohs. Seti I ruled during the 19th dynasty, a period known as the New Kingdom, 1300 years after the Great Pyramid was built and 1000 years before Europeans arrived. Without conclusive evidence, some commentators suggest that Seti I or his son Rameses II is the Pharaoh of Moses that appears in the religious texts of each of the Abrahamic faiths. While those theories can never be resolved, it is clear that Seti I was a significant ruler during a period of imperial strength, and the evidence of this can be seen in what Seti I preserved for his afterlife.

The people of Kemet had an intricate theology, and since the earliest pharaohs, rulers positioned themselves in close proximity to their gods. Much of what we know about life during this time has been discovered through how they prepared for death or worship. The tomb of Seti I, located in the Valley of the Kings in Luxor, is regarded as the most astonishing of all. The walls and ceilings, preserved in their original form, are adorned with colorful depictions of Seti's reign, ancient beliefs about the hereafter, and physical characteristics of the people. In particular, the bright medium brown skin and curly hair of the people of Kemet are unmistakable. For my group of travelers, it was as if we were looking into a mirror, as their pigmentation and phenotype resembled ours. The walls of the burial chamber describe the nightly journey of the sun-god through the underworld as he passes twelve gates, representing each hour of the night. The belief in an afterlife for the pharaoh is connected to the rising of a new day, and this collection of trials is called the Book of Gates. Arguably, the most important scene, which appears in at least three other tombs, is called the Table of Nations. In it, we see Ancient Egyptians as they saw themselves and the world, distinct from others by either nation, religion, or color. The medium brown Ancient Egyptians are followed by an image representing fair-toned Asians, dark brown Nubians, and light brown Libyans. Whiteness did not exist, and people believed to be white would not enter the story of humanity for another 1000 years.

The formative years are critical to developing a child's emotional intelligence, and of all the emotions elementary school children learn to recognize, pride may require the most instruction. Adults do not need to describe happiness or sadness; infants experience these emotions internally, and we only need to provide the language as they grow older, allowing their initial feelings to become more complex and nuanced. The same can be said for anger, fear, and surprise. But children experience pride externally. The first proud moment requires an explicit response: a smile from a parent, a high five, a hug, or a loud cheer. The deeper the pronouncement, the deeper the feeling. As we learn what makes others proud, we seek more of that affirmation, and eventually we discover things about ourselves that feed our self-pride. Schoolchildren take great pride in their work at an early age, and adults are extremely careful about building their confidence. Confident children will have unshakable pride in themselves and in what they can do. They learn never to let anyone or any outcome take away their pride. Similarly, a people must take pride in their work, to understand it, defend it, and pass it down.

In January 2025, I received a warm message and an invitation to return to Florida. A staff member at Fessenden Elementary contacted me with the following note. "We have confirmed a date for our Legacy Day this year: February 27th. Secondly, the school district is at it again, trying to close down Fessenden. I am attaching this link for the recent board meeting."

I followed the link and watched every second of the four-hour school board meeting. Each of Marion County's five districts was represented by an elected official serving a four-year term, and together they were responsible for school operations across the county. The final item of the meeting was rezoning—the technical term for school closings or redistributing students between schools. Stephen Ayres, Director of Student Assignment and Records, presented an update and a slate of recommendations. Specifically, Mr. Ayres recommended that the former Evergreen Elementary not be rezoned until 2027 to prevent the possibility of relocating nearly two dozen students for a third time. Citing low enrollment, the school board voted to close Evergreen Elementary in 2021, resulting in a reassignment of students. The facility reopened in 2022 as an early childhood learning academy, and another shuffle of students occurred. At the time, Marion County residents had a hand in deciding the school's name. They voted to bestow the honor on Edmond Fordham, a retired Black educator, school leader, US veteran, and community organizer.

With the door open, board member Dr. Sarah James, whose district includes the historic Fessenden Academy campus, recommended *offlining* Fessenden Elementary and possibly converting it into an early learning academy, community center, or museum. In Dr. James's vision, closing Fessenden Elementary could allow for various options at the site, including expanded park access, recreational opportunities, and health services for Marion County residents. In her words, "Taking it back to a level of what Fessenden was in the beginning, which was Fessenden Academy and serving students in a different capacity while also serving the community." Another board member concurred with Dr. James and commented, "I believe that the property at Fessenden Elementary School is the perfect location for a special needs shelter, there's vacant land there that could be used regionally. I can see it as a collaboration between the county and state, and our role would be the donation of the land."

This all felt painfully familiar. I have seen gentrification turn public schools into condominiums and parking garages. I have seen eminent domain uproot neighborhoods. I have seen the good, bad, and ugly aftermath of busing and rezoning. Conversely, I have also seen private wealth maintain pristine grounds and boost enrollment in some of the country's most remote independent schools. In large part, pride is a matter of ownership, sovereignty, and possession. The 1951 sale of Fessenden Academy's campus to Marion County was the first strike that stripped away control. However, the alumni of Fessenden Academy and Fessenden High School, as well as the many graduates of Fessenden Elementary, had the land to call their own. They had a school to which they could return and memorialize a transcendent legacy. That was pride. School board members had many compelling reasons to close Fessenden, namely the net financial impact of enrollment and the cost of upkeep. Other board members urged caution with their statements. "Fessenden has always been a place for education when there was no other access. So, honoring that pretty sacred place is top of mind for me in any vote I make." The lone board member of African descent, Mr. Eric Cummings, redirected attention to Mr. Ayres's original recommendation and echoed restraint regarding Fessenden. "Be cautious in how you proceed because if you proceed the wrong way, you're going to get a war you're not ready for."

Ultimately, the board chair confirmed that a vote would be necessary to determine the future of Fessenden Elementary. The community's only role would be to advocate for whether education, in some form, should continue at the treasured site, but the official decision to remain a Marion County public school rested in the hands of the five board members. From a distance, the situation seemed bleak. I felt the panic and worry among Fessenden supporters. As I watched the meeting unfold, arguments in favor of closing the school were well-developed and followed conventional logic. That is, if one saw Fessenden divorced of all its prominence, and the history of the county, state, and nation.

The most threatening factor was a pending multi-million-dollar budget shortfall. I knew enough to know that I did not have all the particulars. I wondered to myself, why not keep Fessenden open and rezone students there? I was mildly aware that board member Dr. Sarah James had a personal connection to the school she proposed for current Fessenden students, as it was a newer building, and according to her, the county could serve them better there. The fear of losing Fessenden was real, and to make matters worse, it was 2025. The political reality included the inauguration of President Donald J. Trump and a sweeping conservative platform, entitled Project 2025, that threatened the existence of the Department of Education, the teaching of diversity, equity, and inclusion (DEI), and access to federal funding for anyone opposed to this agenda.

In late February, I returned to Marion County for the Fessenden Legacy Day event with considerable alarm. Seeing the school again, perhaps for the final time, was a priority, as was my hope of seeing the many community elders who welcomed me so graciously before. Along with my excitement, I carried a measure of grief. The passing of Dr. Gilbert Raiford and the illness of Mr. Whitfield Jenkins, two men from whom I had taken guidance and encouragement as I began researching three years ago, added an urgency and a sense of regret to my visit. How I wish I could have gifted each of them a copy of this book when they were well enough to give me feedback. Instead, I wanted nothing more than to deliver something of quality that would bring support to Fessenden Elementary and honor the few living members of the Academy era.

In comparison to my first trip, the program involved fewer alumni and had far fewer elders in attendance. The audience reflected the diversity of the school, and they were treated to a student performance, a Black History mobile museum, and several speeches. I initially assumed the changes were due to the age and health of many of the alumni. I later confirmed that Fessenden Elementary staff worked tirelessly to revive the program and center it for the students, which prompted the ultimate question: how does one teach Black history in a state that has banned books?

To know it, to understand it, to defend it, and to pass it down. This is how pride becomes a legacy, and the team of administrators, teachers, and staff members, led by Principal Stacey Newmones, was quietly and effectively planting seeds for the next generation. We were still weeks away from the decision on Fessenden's future, but I left Florida with new information and a new charge. The state's crackdown on DEI created genuine anxiety among teachers; books had been removed from the library, and the risk of teaching certain lessons was too great to ignore. This is where knowing Fessenden's legacy can remedy the restriction on an honest telling of US history. In my remarks to the audience, I discussed the early Fessendens and highlighted the abolitionist Samuel Fessenden and his children. I draw a parallel between his actions and those of Ferdinand Stone Fessenden, despite having very different careers and no evidence to suggest that the two men ever met. I asked the audience to consider why their stories, and many others like them, are not discussed in the classroom. With the possibility of Marion County School Board members present, I wanted to make one final point. When Ferdinand signed ownership over to the American Missionary Association (AMA), his will clearly stated that he wished for the Union School and the surrounding land to be used for Black education.

It did not take long for the dots to connect. Did the deed of sale between Marion County Public Schools and the AMA stipulate that Fessenden Academy remain a school? If so, that might compel certain Board members to change course. Several attendees approached me after my remarks with this very question in mind, and it seemed that they were actively investigating. It also seemed obvious. Given all that I have read about the Academy, from Joseph Wiley to John A. Buggs, the AMA, and Florida, it made sense that someone would contractually ensure the land would always be a place for advanced learning. Previously, I had not considered searching for this specific detail, but keeping Fessenden Elementary open could absolutely hinge on the wording of a nearly seventy-five-year-old document. Returning to Boston, I had this new burning question, and an answer to an old lingering one.

The day after the Legacy event, faculty member Amy Watkins showed me through the archives at Fessenden Elementary. The relevant files all fit within a few legal boxes, and we reviewed each piece of paperwork together. Whether the Fessendens in Massachusetts knew of a school bearing their family name in Florida had been an unanswered question from the beginning. The answer is likely no, and a series of letters dating back to 1980 provides a clue. Edward Snowden d'Avi was an Ocala-based architect contracted to remove a number of buildings on the former campus of Fessenden Academy. In 1980, fourteen years before Fessenden Academy earned recognition in the National Register of Historical Places, d'Avi wrote to Florida's Bureau of Historic Sites, connecting Fessenden Academy to The Fessenden School in Massachusetts, and requesting information that could "prevent the potential destruction of perhaps the oldest black school in Florida." Later that year, d'Avi received a return letter from Hart Fessenden, in which Hart explained that someone at the Academy had written to him previously about his connection to Ferdinand. However, at the time, a full name was not provided. Mr. d'Avi's letter contained details that allowed Hart to find the connection between the family lines, and ultimately, he discovered the distinction between the two Fessenden schools.

At the time of Hart's letter, The Fessenden School had only ten Black graduates. I no longer had to wonder if knowing about Fessenden Academy, or the name of the first Black student to enroll, would have been meaningful to those young men – mainly because I have seen the pride this knowledge has bestowed on current students. Every child needs to know that they are not alone, and deserves to know who came first. And, Fessenden's first Black graduate, Stuart Perry, would officially return to campus for the first time to tell us. We planned his visit to align with the annual VOICE cookout, which has become a ceremonial gathering for Black students, faculty, and families, and a rite of passage for departing students. Perry, who graduated as the-only, spoke to an audience of over fifty VOICE boys, pre-kindergarten to grade nine, and shared his Fessenden story. His parents were not there to see his return, nor were his classmates and former teachers. However, supporting him throughout this landmark occasion were his son and a close cousin. As fate would have it, what began for young Stuart as his parents' decision to attend Fessenden returned him to campus as an answer to a current parent's question. If I have learned anything in my study of schools, it is that Black children must have pride in who they are. And Black parents, with no guarantees in this land of ours, have historically placed their faith in schools.

Around this same time, I also took a leap of faith and reached out to school board member Dr. Sarah James. I knew that she was leading the charge that could close Fessenden Elementary, and I knew that the decision was looming. We spoke for about thirty minutes on the phone, and I mainly listened as she described the issues. In my mind, I fit the profile of an outside agitator, so I intended to take a different posture. I did not doubt that a fiscal decision of preference between closing Fessenden or another school should not be a 2025 analysis, but rather an accounting from 1865 to 2025 at the very least. I thought my research could help, but I had no idea if our differing worldviews and politics would allow either of us to be open-minded. Nearing the end of the call, I asked about Fessenden Elementary's future. Dr. James responded, "You haven't heard. I thought that was why you asked to speak." For weeks, I was in a research and writing bubble and had emerged with no record of the sale of the Academy to Marion County. I had not received any updates from the community elders either, so I grew ever more anxious. After hearing all the issues facing the school district, I did not expect great news. Instead, Dr. James explained that the Board did not vote on rezoning. The public outcry to keep Fessenden Elementary open was significant, and for now, the indelible legacy would continue. As the call ended, I was pleasantly shocked but not surprised. There is something special about that place. It is the land, it is the people, and it is the land that allows generations to return.

As I witness a similar intergenerational exchange beginning at the Fessenden in the North, it was not a mystery after all. There was no conspiracy to keep the stories of the two Fessenden schools as distant from each other as their geographical locations dictate. There is no structural racism to see here, not as we conclude; there is only memory, pride, and school. I pray that this story pulls back the curtain and reveals how little we remember, how selective memory becomes collective pride, and how schools achieve this most effectively with race.

ACKNOWLEDGEMENTS

All praise is due to Allah, Lord of mankind and creator of the world. After giving thanks to God, my family deserves the most acknowledgement. I have wanted nothing more than to make my parents, and their parents, and their parents, and all past generations proud. To my mother, Annette Scott, I owe you more than I can repay, so I have tried to honor everything you have taught me in my actions. To the generation prior, my grandmother, Anna Singletary, whom I spent the most time with, what I can not repay, I will pay it forward. To my father, Imam Khary, my siblings, Anwar, Jamal, Ali, and Ameena, and my nephews, Atif is a powerful legacy. I have done my best to hold it high, and together we will carry it further. To my Khadijah, Bayaan, and Salih, I owe you everything, including my gratitude and a profound apology. This story has occupied time and labor that have taken me away from you physically, mentally, and emotionally. And, despite my best intentions, it has been taxing on you most directly. I do not think I will write this much again, ever, because of how isolating it felt. However, each of you made it ever so easy because of your patience with me and your confidence in me. Thank you.

It is impossible to imagine completing this project without the support of The Fessenden School, Fessenden Elementary, Fessenden Academy Alumni, and the Fessenden family itself. Namely, Mandy Brauer, the granddaughter of Frederick James Fessenden, has passionately followed my journey, reading my chapters and offering a uniquely personal perspective. I am also the beneficiary of significant organizational work that preceded my appointment at The Fessenden School in 2020. Since then, a global pandemic, the racial uprising following the murder of George Floyd, and an all-out political assault on DEI have made for unprecedented times at schools. Likewise, there was no playbook to consult when I suggested my plan for research, teaching, and writing to Fessenden colleagues. While it has been my intention to be honest, compassionate, and respectful, I must acknowledge that sharing this story may evoke strong and possibly oppositional feelings in some. So it is with an abundance of caution that I have decided to offer my thanks to those colleagues who aided me in more ways than I can list, in person, rather than here.

I recall the day when I spoke to a host of Black faculty. I showed each of you images of Fesseden Academy from Tulane University's Amistad Research Center, and I knew from your reaction then that I had to tell this story. Likewise, prospective Black families, candidates of color, and Black alumni who return all have a similar response. As former and future students and Black educators at Fessenden, what was understood did not need an explanation. The parents of VOICE boys throughout my time are too numerous to name, but I must acknowledge your impact as well. I certainly understand that telling a different story about Fessenden would have ripple effects. I will take credit for any mistakes, miscalculations, or unintended consequences, but if there's any good to come, I have reached this far by inspiration, not isolation. My one desire was for each VOICE boy to know that they were not alone, and that effort began over twenty years ago, before I arrived. Lavette Coney, I hope this work honors what you envisioned and endeavored to create for Fessy boys.

Mr. Whitfield and Mrs. Loretta Jenkins were the first to greet me in Florida, and they paved the way for me to meet most of the alumni community. In particular, it was an honor to have spent time with Ms. Demoris Rhodes and Dr. Gilbert Raiford from the Fessenden Academy Era. The memories you shared with me are treasured and cherished. To Mr. Johnny Grimes, your initial invite to the Reunion in 2023 was the catalyst for much of what followed. Having read so much about the early years of the Union School, I am grateful to Linda Ward and Larry Rose for sharing primary source documents about their ancestor, Father Thomas Ward. Similarly, I want to thank Principal Stacey Newmones and Amy Watkins, who graciously allowed me to access the archives located at Fessenden Elementary. As a newcomer, I was treated like an honored guest by all Fessenden staff, families, and students, and for that, I say thank you.

Doubt can cause paralysis, and few things have threatened my confidence more than taking an intellectual risk, without a mentor and formal training in a new discipline. Narrative writing, archival research, and oral history are technical crafts that I have only begun to learn. I started with an essay and convinced myself that I had to tell the most complete story possible. Khadijah Campbell was there from day one and fueled my ambition. Onaje Woodbine made me believe that I had a story to tell. Marisa Pagano edited my chapters over the course of three years. Erik Wade helped improve my composition, Hannah Lim suggested new angles and key revisions, Corey Dupree showed love and introduced me to Danielle Marietta, who brings this publication to life. I would be remiss not to acknowledge all of my teachers, from my parents to those at James Rhoades Elementary, Conwell Middle, and Central High School. My professors at Cheyney and

Delaware State, as well as institutions like the Jawala Scouts and the Quba Institute, have shaped my view of the world and my purpose in life.

In my office, next to a framed portrait of Fessenden Academy students, sits the African Studies Framework poster. To Dr. Greg Carr and the other architects, your framework enabled me to properly answer a question that a brilliant student asked me many years ago, when I was the Dean of Multicultural Affairs at Phillips Exeter Academy. How does one decolonize the mind at a predominantly white school? At the time, the question and my response were equally rhetorical as we both understood the dilemma. However, the framework provides an active mechanism to cleanse the palate and rewire our thinking. These ideas are present in Race Pride School Pride, and I owe a measure of credit to many predecessors.

Finally, I want to acknowledge us. We stand on many shoulders.

End Notes

[1] Dolin, E.J., *Furs, Fortune and Empire, The Epic History of the Fur Trade in America*

[2] Whitmore, W. H., *Colonial Laws of Massachusetts: reprinted...the Body of Liberties 1641,* 1889, p. 53, Boston Public Library

[3] Cave, Alfred, *The Pequot War,* 1996, p.161

[4] Facing History & Ourselves, *Religion in Colonial America: Trends, Regulations, and Beliefs,* last updated March 14, 2016

[5] Pestana, Carla, *Quakers and Baptists in Colonial Massachusetts,* 1991, 2004

[6] Dunning, A. E., *Congregationalists in America...origin, belief, polity, growth, and work,* 1884, New York Public Library

[7] Peters, Paula, Mashpee, Wampanoag, *The Great Dying: God's Will or Unfortunate Circumstance,* National Museum of the American Indian

[8] Fessenden, Edwin Allan, *The Fessenden Family in America Vol. 1,* p. 2-5

[9] Maine Historical Society and American Historical Society, *Maine, A History Vol. 2,* p.383

[10] Cooper, James, *Tenacious of Their Liberties: The Congregationalists in Colonial Massachusetts,* 1999

[11] Holmes, Thomas, J., *Cotton Mather: A Bibliography of his Works,* Newton Mass.: Crofton Publishing Co. 1974

[12] Mather, Cotton, Mather, Increase, *The Wonders of the Invisisble World: Being an Account of the Tryals...A Farther Account of the Tryals,* London: John Russell Smith, 1692, Introduction

[13] Mather, Cotton, *Diary of Cotton Mather,* 1706, 13d. 10m. (Library of Mass. Historical Society)

[14] Koo, Kathryn S., *Stranger in the House of God: Cotton Mather, Onesimus, and an Experiment in Christian Slaveholding,* American Antiquarian Society, 2007, p. 147-149

[15] Boylston, Arthur, *The Origins of Inoculation*, Journal of the Royal Society of Medicine vol. 105,7 (2012): 309-13. doi:10.1258/jrsm.2012.12k044

[16] Mather, Cotton, *Diary of Cotton Mather,* Massachusetts Historical Society, August, 1716, p. 383

[17] Ross, Emily, *Report on Members of Color at Old South Church and Members who Enslaved People of Color*, Revised November 2021

[18] Fessenden, Edwin Allan, *The Fessenden Family in America Vol. 1*, p. 108

[19] Sewall, Samuel, *The Selling of Joseph: A Memorial,* 1700, Massachusetts Historical Society

[20] Goodell, Abner Cheney, *The Trail and Execution for Petit Treason of Mark and Phillis, Slaves of Capt. John Codman*, 1883, Cambrige, J. Wilson and Son, The John Hopkins University Sheridan Library

[21] Letter from Paul Revere to Jeremy Belknap, circa 1798, Massachusetts Historical Society

[22] Fessenden, Edwin Allan, *The Fessenden Family in America Vol. 2*, pg 473-478

[23] *Fryeburg: An historical sketch.* Fryeburg, ME: Pequawket Press, 1938.

[24] Evans, Simeon A., *The Descendants of David Evans of Charelston, Massachusetts*, 1893, p.9

[25] Eastman, Tom, *The Surprising Story of Slavery in Fryeburg*, The Conway Daily Sun, December 2022

[26] Fessenden, Edwin Allan, *The Fessenden Family in America Vol. 2* p. 479-480

[27] Hall, Prince, *To the Honorable Counsel and House of Representatives for the State of Massachusetts Bay in General Court assembled January 13, 1777,* Collections of the Massachusetts Historical Society, 5th ser., 3 (1877) Negro Petitions for Freedom, p. 1

[28] Hall, Prince, *Petition of Prince Hall to the Massachusetts General Court,* Febuary, 27, 1788, Jeremy Belknap Papers, Massachusetts Historical Society

[29] Jefferson, Thomas, *Notes on the State of Virginia,* Boston, Lily, and Wait, 1832, New York Public Library, p. 146

[30] Hill, Tony, *Ethnicity and Education, The politics of black education,* Boston Review, October, 1981

[31] *Old Deluder Satan Law of 1647*, Laws and Liberties of Massachusetts, Reprinted from the 1648 Edition in the Henry E. Huntington Library

[32] Apetheker, Hebert, *A Documentary History of the Negro People in the United States,* New York, Citadel Press, 1951, p.19-20

[33] Easton, Hosea, *A Treatise on the Intellectual Character, and Civil and Political Condition of Colored of the United States: and the prejudice exercised against them,* Boston, MA., 1837, p. 40-42

[34] Mills, ShaVonte', *An African School for African Americans: Black Demand for Education in Antebellum Boston,* History of Education Quarterly, Vol. 61, Special Issue 4, November 2021

[35] Schultz, Stanley, *The Culture Factory, Boston Public Schools, 1789-1860,* New York, Oxford University Press, 1973, p. 159-162

[36] Op. Cit

[37] White, Authur O., *The Black Leadership Class and Education in Antebellum Boston,* Journal of Negro Education, Vol. 42, No.4, Autumn, 1973, p. 505-506

[38] Bower, Beth Ann; Rushing, Byron, *The African Meeting House: The Center for the 19th Century Afro-American Community in Boston,* Archeological Perspectives on Ethnicity in America. Vol. 1. New York, 1980.

[39] Mills, ShaVonte', An *African School for African Americans: Black Demand for Education in Antebellum Boston,* History of Education Quarterly, Vol. 61, Special Issue 4, November 2021

[40] Levesque, George, *Before Integration: The Forgotten Years of Jim Crow Education in Boston,* The Journal of Negro Education, Vol. 48, No. 2, Spring 1979, p. 114-116

[41] Middleton, George, *Petition of George Middleton and 66 Blacks, "To The Honorable Gentlemen of the School Committee of the Town of Boston,* City of Boston School Committee Minutes manuscript: 1792-1905, vol.1, Boston Public Library

[42] Davis, Gerald Nelson, *Massachusetts Black and the Quest for Education, 1638 - 1860,* University of Massachusetts Amherst, 1977, Doctoral Dissertations 1896 - February 2014

[43] Kendrick, Stephen; Kendrick, Paul, *Sarah's Long Walk, The Free Blacks of Boston and How Their Struggle for Equality Changed America,* Beacon Press, Boston, 2004, p. 73

[44] School Committee Records, V (1846-1849) August 11, 1848; Sept. 12, 1849; 2, 1849; Report

of a Special Committee of the Grammar School Board (1849)

[45] Sumner, Charles, *Argument of Charles Sumner Esq. Against the Constitutionality of Separate Colored Schools*, in the case of Sara Roberts v. City of Boston, Before the Supreme Court of Massachusetts, December 4, 1849

[46] Souther, Samuel, *The Centinnial Celebration of the Settlement of Fryeburg, Maine,* 1864, Tyler and Seagrave, Worcester, MA.

[47] Mann, Horace, *The Massachusetts System of Common Schools: Tenth Annual Report of the First Secretary of the Massachusetts Board of Education,* 1849, Library of Congress, p.10

[48] Barrow, John Stuart, *Fryeburg, An Historical Sketch,* Pequawket Press, 1983, p. 118-119

[49] Op. Cit., p. 123-124

[50] Fessenden, Edwin Allan, *The Fessenden Family in America Vol. 1*, p. 507

[51] Mallett, Richard P., and Roger Ray, *Maine Crusades and Crusaders, 1830-1850 and Addenda*. Maine History 17, 4 (1978): p. 183-214

[52] Fessenden, Edwin Allan, *The Fessenden Family in America Vol. II*, p. 507

[53] Kidder, David, *Owning Our History: First Church and Race 1636-1873*, First Church in Cambridge Congregational, 2011, p. 9-10

[54] Warrant for Habeas Corpus; 9/21/1839; United States v. Cinque and the Africans; Case Files, 1790 - 1911; Records of District Courts of the United States, Record Group 21; National Archives at Boston, Waltham, MA.

[55] Linder, Doug, *Stamped with Glory: Lewis Tappan and the Africans of the Amistad,* 2008, Available at SSRN: http://dx.doi.org/10.2139/ssrn.1109114

[56] Fessenden, Samuel to Samuel E. Sewall, 5 July 1844, Robie-Sewall family papers, Massachusetts Historical Society.

[57] Fessenden, Edwin Allan, *The Fessenden Family in America Vol. II*, pg. 817

[58] Douglass, Frederick, *Life and Times of Frederick Douglass,* Hartford, CT., Park Publishing, 1881, p. 475

[59] Fessenden, Francis, *Life and Public Service of WIlliam Pitt Fessenden, U.S. Senator from Maine 1854-1869 Vol. 1,* Houghton, Mifflin and Company, 1907, p. 37

[60]National Park Service, Independence National Historical Park Archives, Castillo De San Marcos, *African Americans in St. Augustine 1565-1821,* October 2, 2023 https://www.nps.gov/casa/learn/historyculture/african-americans-in-st-augustine-1565-1821.htm

[61] Op. Cit

[62] Op. Cit

[63] Smith, Julia Floyd, *Slavery and Plantation Growth in Antebellum Florida, 1821-1860,* University of FLorida Press, 2017, p. 27

[64] *Biographical Souvenir of the States of Georgia And Florida: Containing Biographical Sketches of the Representative Public, And Many Early Settled Families In These States.* Chicago: F.A. Battey & Co., 1889, p. 569

[65] Smith, Julia Floyd, *Slavery and Plantation Growth in Antebellum Florida, 1821-1860,* University of FLorida Press, 2017, p. 222

[66] Seaman, Bruce, *To Succeed Where Others Failed: The Untold Story of the Marshall Plantation Raid,* 2022

[67] Murray, Vince, *Captain J. J. Dickison: Marion County's Civil War Hero,* Ocala Star Banner, April 25, 2008

[68] Herman, S.H.S, *The Jacksonville Expedition,* The Christian Recorder, April, 22 1865

[69] Klustens, Claire Prechtel, *Civil War Confederate Slave Payroll Records,* NGS Magazine, April-June 2019, Vol. 45, No. 2

[70] *Thomas Benjamin Ward Pension Application*, June 10, 1908, obtained from Ward Family Records

[71] United States Continental Congress, et al. An ordinance for ascertaining the mode of disposing of lands in the Western Territory: Be it ordained by the United States in Congress assembled, that the territory ceded by individual states to the United States, which has been purchased of the Indian inhabitants, shall be disposed of in the following manner. [New York: s.n, 1785] Online Text. Retrieved from the Library of Congress, <www.loc.gov/item/90898224/>

[72] Ordinance for the Government of the Territory of the United States North-West of the River Ohio; 7/13/1787; Miscellaneous Papers of the Continental Congress, 1774 - 1789; Records of the Continental and Confederation Congresses and the Constitutional Convention, Record Group 360; National Archives Building, Washington, DC

[73] H.R. Rep. No. 312, 21st Cong., 1st Sess. (1830)

[74] Smith, Julia Floyd, *Slavery and Plantation Growth in Antebellum Florida, 1821-1860,* University of FLorida Press, 2017, p. 189

[75] Gray, Lewis Cecil, *History of Agriculture in Southern United States to 1860,* The Carnegie Institute of Washington, 1933, p. 635

[76] Cochran, Thomas, *History of Public School in Florida,* Press of New Era Printing Company, 1921, pg 28

[77] Life and Public Services of William Pitt Fessenden, U.S. Senator from Maine 1854-1864, Francis Fessenden, 1907, p. 29

[78] Bush, George Gary, *The History of Education in Florida,* George Bush, Washington Government Printing Office, 1889, p. 23-24

[79] DeBoer, Clara Merritt, *His Truth is Marching On African Americans Who Taught the Freedmen for the American Missionary Association 1861-1877*, 1995, p. 5

[80] Christian Abolition: The American Missionary Association and the Florida Negro, Joe Richardson, The Journal of Negro Education, Winter, 1971, Vol.40, No. 1 p. 35-44

[81] West, Earle H. *The Peabody Education Fund and Negro Education, 1867-1880.* History of Education Quarterly, vol. 6, no. 2, 1966, p. 3–21

[82] Rosen, F. Bruce, *The Influence of the Peabody Fund on Education in Reconstruction Florida*, Florida Historical Quarterly: Vol. 55 : No. 3 , Article 6, 1976

[83] Fessenden, Edwin Allan, *The Fessenden Family in America Vol. 1*, p.323

[84] Beard, August F., *Sketches from the South*, The American Missionary Vol.51, 1897

[85] Wiley, Joseph, *A School in the Black Belt of Florida*, The American Missionary Vol. 58, December 1904, p.324

[86] Richardson, Joe, *Joseph Wiley: A Black Florida Educator*, Florida Historical Quarterly Vol. 71 No.4

[87] Odom, Jennifer, *Fessenden Elementary School Grads Flock to Ocala*, Ocala StarBanner, July 2011

[88] Wiley, Joseph, *Fessenden Academy and Industrial School Catalog, 1900-1901*, State Library of Florida, Federal Documents Collection

[89] Richardson, Joe, *Joseph Wiley: A Black Florida Educator*, Florida Historical Quarterly Vol. 71 No.4

[90] Wiley, Joseph, *Fessenden Academy and Industrial School Catalog, 1900-1901*, State Library of Florida, Federal Documents Collection

[91] Notes section, The American Missionary, Vol. 60, 1906 p.187

[92] Note and Comment section, The American Missionary, Vol 63 1909 p.248

[93] Wiley, Joseph, *How They Grow*, The American Missionary 1914, Vol 68 p.216

[94] Richardson, Joe, *Joseph Wiley: A Black Florida Educator,* Florida Historical Quarterly Vol. 71 No.4

[95] Fessenden, Katherine, *The Fessenden School 1903-1967*, 1971, p. 6.

[96] Hyde, Henry Knight, *Charles McEwen Hyde: A Memorial*, (Ware, Mass.: Eddy Press., 1901) p. 30.

[97] Nellist, George F., *Men of Hawaii:Volume IV.*, (The Honolulu Star-Bulletin, Limited, 1930) p. 85-87.

[98] Brown, M.A. *Facing the Spears of Change: The Life and Legacy of I. K. P. ʻĪʻī*, (University of Hawaii Press, 2014).

[99] Fessenden, Katharine, *The Fessenden School 1903-1967*, 1971 p. 23

[100] Fessenden, Katharine *The Fessenden School 1903-1967*, 1971, p.76

[101] Eleanor Roosevelt Papers, *Radio Address, December 7, 1941 (Attack on Pearl Harbor),* The George Washington University, Columbian College of Arts and Sciences

[102] Fessenden, Katharine *The Fessenden School, 1903-1967*, p. 80

[103] David W. Blight, *Race and Reunion: The Civil War in American Memory*, (Harvard University Press, 2002), p. 69-71.

[104] Esteban Bustillos, "Meet the Boston Native at the Center of the Tuskegee Airmen Mural at Boston Logan Airport," *WGBH*, March 2024.

[105] Eleanor Roosevelt, "My Day, April 1, 1941," *The Eleanor Roosevelt Papers Digital Edition* (2017).

[106] "Who's Who in Our Faculty," *The Dentoscope*, Vol. 21: Iss. 2, Article 9. Howard University, 1941.

[107] Giles, Mark S., *Special Focus: Dr. Anna Julia Cooper, 1858-1964, Teacher, Scholar, and Timeless Womanist,* The Journal of Negro Education, Vol. 75, No. 4 (Fall, 2006): 621-634.

[108] Cooper, Anna J., *A Voice from the South*, 1892.

[109] Hurston, Zore Neale, *Their Eyes Were Watching God.*

[110] Fuller Jr., Neely, *The United Independent Compensatory Code/System/Concept: A Textbook/Workbook for Thought, Speech and/or Action for Victims of Racism (White Supremacy)*, 1984.

[111] Banner Staff, *Dr. Martin Luther King Jr.'s Boston Legacy*, Bay State Banner, January 16, 2020.

[112] *Martin Luther King's Address to the Mass State Legislature*, Bay State Banner, January 20, 2014.

[113] Ladson-Billings, Gloria, *But That's Just Good Teaching! The Case for Culturally Relevant Pedagogy,* Theory Into Practice, Vol. 34, No. 3, 1995: 159–65. *JSTOR,* http://www.jstor.org/stable/1476635.

[114] *American Missionary,* Vol. 47, October 1893, 308.

[115] Richardson, Joe, *"Florida Black Codes,"* The Florida Historical Quarterly 47, no. 4 (1969) 371.

[116] Washington, Booker T., "Atlanta Exposition Speech," [Manuscript/Mixed Material, 1895] Retrieved from the Library of Congress.

[117] Records of the Assistant Commissioner and Subordinate Field Offices for the State of Florida, Freedmans Bureau, 1865–1872, p.5.

[118] Wakefield, Laura, *Set A Light In A Dark Place: Teachers Of Freedmen In Florida,* 1863–1874, 2004, p. 59-60.

[119] Richardson, Joe, *An Evaluation of Freedman's Bureau in Florida,* The Florida Historical Quarterly 4, no. 3, 1963, 15-16.

[120] Richardson, Joe, *Joseph L. Wiley: A Black Florida Educator,* The Florida Historical Quartrely 71, no. 3, 1993.

[121] Jackson Jr., David. H., *Booker T. Washington's Tour of the Sunshine State,* March 1912, The Florida Historical Quarterly 81, no. 3(2003) 268.

[122] Richardson, Joe; Jones, Maxine D., *Education for Liberation,* 2009, pg 43-44.

[123] *American Missionary,* Vol. 69, 1915.

[124] "Lynching in America: From 'Popular Justice' to Racial Terror, Equal Justice Initiative," 2017, p. 41.

[125] Tonlay, Stewart E.; Beck, E. M., *A Festival of Violence: An Analysis of Southern Lynchings, 1882–1930,* 1995, p. 38.

[126] Vandiver, Margaret *Lethal Punishment,* 2005, p. 70-74.

[127] M. D. Potter to NAACP, June 25, 1937; Papers of the NAACP, Part 7, The Anti-Lynching Campaign, 1912–1953.

[128] Newton, Michael, *The Invisible Empire: The KKK in Florida,* 2001, p. 41.

[129] *American Missionary*, May 1917, p. 98-99.

[130] Bartley, A. Abel; Winsboro, Irvin, *Reading, Writing, and Racism: The Long and Troubling History of Segregated Schools in Florida,* Hawaii University International Conferences, January 2015, p. 9.

[131] Sheats, William, *Biennial Report of the Superintendent of Public Instruction of the State of Florida for the Two Years Ending June 30, 1918*, p. 28-29.

[132] Rosen, Bruce, *The Influence of the Peabody Fund on Education in Reconstruction Florida*, The Florida Historically Quarterly 55, no. 3, 1977, p. 314.

[133] Cawthorn, W. S., *Biennial Report of the Superintendent of Public Instruction of the State of Florida For the Two Years Ending June 30, 1928*, 221-240.

[134] Richardson, Joe; Jones, Maxine D. *Education for Liberation*, 2009, p. 62, p. 71.

[135] *The American Missionary* 79, no. 4, April, 1925, 11.

[136] Du Bois, W. E. B. (William Edward Burghardt) 1868–1963. *Letter from W. E. B. Du Bois to the American Missionary Association*, April 26, 1930. W. E. B. Du Bois Papers (MS 312). Special Collections and University Archives, University of Massachusetts Amherst Libraries.

[137] Du Bois, W. E. B. *The Education of Black People, Ten Critiques 1906–1960*, 1973, p. 70-71, p. 88.

[138] Richardson, Joe; Jones, Maxine D. *Education for Liberation*, 2009, p. 77-78.

[139] Richardson, Joe; Jones, Maxine D. *Education for Liberation*, 2009 p. 198-199.

[140] Buggs, John A. *Resume of Six Years of Educational Experiment*, p. 4-15.

[141] Gibson Jr., Truman K. *Governments Fails Negro Vets: Systemic Denial of Rights Under the GI Bill Scored at Conference, Pittsburg Courier*, April 13, 1946.

[142] Schnur, James A. *Caught in Crossfire: African Americans and Florida's System of Labor During WWII*, Sunland Tribune 19, Article 8, 1993.

[143] Richardson, Joe; Jones, Maxine D. *Education for Liberation*, 2009, p. 96-97.

[144] Richardson, Joe; Jones, Maxine D. *Education for Liberation*, 2009, p. 101-106.

[145] Brownlee, Frederick, *New Day Ascending*, 1946, p.114-120.

[146] Richardson, Joe; Jones, Maxine D. *Education for Liberation*, 2009, p. 113-1124.

[147] Frederick Brownlee, *The American Missionary Association, Yesterday and Tomorrow*, 1950, 68-69.

[148] Richardson, Joe; Jones, Maxine D. *Education for Liberation*, 2009, p. 101-106.

[149] *The Christmas 1951 Murders of Harry T. and Harriette V. Moore, Results of the Attorney General's Investigation, Executive Summary (revised), Charlie Crist,* February 2018.

[150] Brownlee, Frederick, *The American Missionary Association, Yesterday and Tomorrow*, 1950, p. 68-69.

www.ingramcontent.com/pod-product-compliance
Lightning Source LLC
Chambersburg PA
CBHW011236120626
46549CB00009B/3291